I've been fortunate enough to get to know Connie through our work together in mental health. Connie's passion, humility, and integrity in her work are infectious. In *Bring Them Closer*, Connie lets us into the world that she and her family have been living in, and how far they've come in their journey through mental health and healing. Now she wants their journey to help others and change how we view our approach to mental health and strengthening our families. While there's no quick-fix, one-size-fits-all approach, I'm convinced that the stories and principles in this book will be of great encouragement, and great help to those who read it. I'm privileged to recommend this book to individuals, families, and professionals alike. We need people like Connie to change the face of mental health in our families and our communities.

—Andrew Neufeld, Registered Clinical Counsellor, Co-Founder and Executive Director, Alongside You

With courage and conviction, *Bring Them Closer* invites readers to consider that a different way to parent our children is available to us—and it's ultimately rooted in connection. Connie Jakab vulnerably shares her own family's story, while also providing practical tools and steps for those of us who are learning that love is always the best resource we have. This is an excellent book for parents and caregivers who are looking to pursue a different rhythm in their family and home.

—Aundi Kolber, Licensed Professional Counsellor and Author of *Try Softer*

As a mom of older kids (twenty-two, twenty, and seventeen), I can certainly look back at my parenting and name all kinds of things that I did "wrong." In *Bring Them Closer*, parents can find hope and encouragement that their mistakes don't have to be the end of the story. Connie Jakab gives a ton of very helpful advice, isn't afraid to share her struggles, and understands the psychological principles that create safe spaces for our kids. Yes, there were things I would have done differently, and I didn't have kids who struggled with mental health issues, but I still understood that raising strong kids who are happy, healthy contributing members of society is not a task for the fainthearted. Jakab's book will help you understand your priorities in parenting and how being the best version of yourself will help your kids be the best version of themselves as well.

—Stephanie Reeves, Writer and Parent
www.stephreeves.wordpress.com

As a public speaker on mental health, Connie Jakab's compassionate call to courage informs and inspires me in my own parenting. Not only is she enlightening on how to meet our children in their greatest need, but her vulnerability as she interweaves her story into her teaching makes her a trustworthy companion while we navigate our relationships with our children. In an age when anxiety, depression, and suicide in children is at an all-time high, *Bring Them Closer* is a beacon of hope.

—Leah Everson (MDiv), Public Speaker and Writer

Some books teach. Others inspire. This book does both. *Bring Them Closer* is a beautiful tapestry of stories that describe where all parents live—in the tension of wanting to be enough for our children and knowing we are not, even as we continue to try. As that tension gets passed down to our children, we need tools to create a safe place of belonging—for them and us. As Connie describes, "Belonging is one of those things that doesn't come cheap. You can only give it away if you own it yourself deep down." This book has changed me down deep, giving me the freedom to rest fully in the fact that I am not "just a parent," but a person given the gift to change lives: giving gathered bits of grace to release fears, truths to bring comfort, and hope to those in my home. A comrade on the front lines, Connie offers encouragements to embrace the "messy" as we cherish the years gifted to us. My mothering will be changed because of this book and may we all continue to know each of us and our families are loved and held.

—Angie Ryg, M.A.Ed.
Teacher, Speaker, Mother, Founder of Inspire Retreat,
Author of *Clutter Free Simplicity*, and contributor to
(in)courage Women's Devotional Bible and Everbloom

Connie Jakab is one of the bravest women I know. Not only owning her part of the story but entering into it. When parenting peels off layers of our soul and reveals the darkness, it is only those with courage that walk towards it. Connie shares the brutal and beautiful reality of living with a child that rises with mental healing. Learning that healing can only occur if we pull closer to each other. Mamas and papas and caregivers of those we love, you have opened a book that is raw and will let you know you are never alone in those waiting rooms again.

—Sheli Massie, Writer, Speaker, Advocate
for Social Justice and Healing

Bring Them Closer is a vulnerable, convicting, informative and compelling read; a unique blend of captivating personal story, proven professional expertise and grounded faith. Connie Jakab's honesty will arrest you, her humble presentation of how she struggled to hold onto hope while journeying through the realities of many hard-knock life lessons learned will encourage and inspire you, and her ability to contextualize the wisdom of many well-respected voices and make it applicable to your life will greatly assist you. You can't read this book as a parent and not feel simultaneously challenged and encouraged. This book is a timely and needed addition to the library of parenting resources.

—Paul Day, PhD, MFT
Psychotherapist, Clinical Supervisor, Public Speaker, Author

Bring them Closer

Bring
them
Closer

Calling Parents to Courage
through the Mental Health Crisis

Connie Jakab

BRING THEM CLOSER
Copyright © 2020 by Connie Jakab

Printed in Canada

ISBN: 978-1-4866-1972-6
eBook ISBN: 978-1-4866-1973-3

Word Alive Press
119 De Baets Street Winnipeg, MB R2J 3R9
www.wordalivepress.ca

Cataloguing in Publication information can be obtained from Library and Archives Canada.

This book is dedicated to my first loves
—my family—
for all that we have overcome together.
To my boys, you are more courageous than you know.
To my husband, you are an overcomer.
And to every family in the struggle, know that there is hope.

Contents

Introduction

I KNOW MOST PEOPLE SKIP THE INTRODUCTION. WHAT'S THE POINT OF AN INTRODUCTION anyway, am I right?

Trust me, don't skip this one.

I'm so thankful you're joining me on this journey, brave one. This isn't just a book; it's a journey full of discovery, honesty, and hope. I share the social patterns I've noticed in my twenty years of resilience work, along with our own family's personal experience of our son's mental health crisis. The content isn't for the faint of heart. In fact, I'm going to be upfront; it's going to be a hard read at times. When it gets too hard, I want you to push through, because there's a new story waiting for you, your family, and the families around us if we find our courage. I'm calling the adults back to the playing field of our children's lives.

Most of my resilience work has come through the work I've done in schools, starting in lower-income communities with at-risk youth. From there, I expanded into suburbia and noticed something curious. As mental health concerns, such as anxiety and depression, rose as a social norm it seemed to flatline these two seemingly different socio-economic demographics. I saw the same outward manifestations of anxiety and depression in at-risk youth from lower-income communities in suburbia. Even the affluent children showed the same struggles with mental health, but for different reasons.

Early in my career, while I was working in lower-income communities, my colleagues and I would speak about "those families" whose parents weren't home for their kids—families who were broken, who experienced abuse and poverty. We would speak about youth issues and put it back on "those parents" who were divorced, addicted, stricken by poverty, etc. However, the rise of mental illness has unveiled the truth that there's no such thing as "those families." In suburbia and affluent communities behind closed doors, there has been the same abuse, marital conflict, and even *poverty*.

We need to relook at the definition of "poverty." We think it's about being "poor" but it's more about a lack of quality of life. The truth is that our mental health crisis shows us that we are all impoverished. While some may experience homelessness, others are just as impoverished due to living off a line of credit in order to survive—or perhaps just to keep up with what society tells us is "survival."

I have news for suburban folks. A daily Starbucks and an annual trip to Mexico is not "survival." While one youth from the urban ghetto sells drugs in order to help his family pay rent, the other suburban youth is in the corner rocking back and forth from being told their allowance has been put on hold until the credit card has been paid down. Who's really living in lack?

Many times, people who are struggling are those whom we would least expect. CEOs, leaders, people with loads of money, Instagram stars, YouTube "trenders," celebrities, etc. Mental illness doesn't. It truly does show us, once again, that money, success, and popularity don't deliver as much as we are told it does.

We can't speak about mental health without addressing the issue of poverty. What's *your* poverty? This is a question we all must face. We've been putting up with a quality of life that's less than we deserve. The tragedy is that we are putting up with it like "it's just the way it is." Societal issues are there only because we choose to tolerate them. I am sending a wake-up call to our culture. Look around! Our youth are not okay. They are a mirror back to us of the state of our society. As family disconnection has risen, so has youth mental health concerns.

Over the last ten years, I've seen with my very eyes the increase of youth-related anxiety and depression. A study from the University of Calgary, Raising Canada, revealed that in the last decade, fifty-five percent of hospital visits from children and youth have been for mental health-related issues. I'm not sure if we realize the severity of that.

In order for a youth to visit a hospital for a mental health concern, they must have threatened their life. This statistic isn't about a doctor visit for meds or to be referred to a counsellor. To visit a hospital means that a child is in crisis. Fifty-five percent! Just let that sink in for a moment. That's more than broken legs or arms. Our children are not okay. In this same study, they discovered that suicide was the second leading cause of death of children to age seventeen. As of right now 1.2 million children and youth in Canada where I live are affected by mental illness, and only twenty percent of them are receiving the proper treatment.

Seriously, are we awake yet?

One in five youth today struggle with a mental health issue. Every single one of those "one-in-fives" is connected to a parent, a caregiver, a teacher, or a grandparent who is more than likely feeling lost about how to help that child. Our issue as caregivers isn't that we don't *want* to do something; it's that we don't know *how*.

This book is going to show you how.

How do you bring a child who is depressed to recovery?

How do you bring a suicidal youth to life?

How do you bring a child drowning in anxiety to peace?

You're about to find out.

In just the past three to five years, I have noticed youth are struggling to know how to connect with others. Much of the work I do in school circles leave youth mentioning the experience of having to face and look at others as "awkward."

Honestly, I'm done with us putting band-aids on today's mental health problems. I'm realizing that answers to poverty, family breakdown, and social issues in schools like bullying are not going to be solved alone by government or organizations, but by the awakening of people like you and me. For families and educators to be given the tools to make change happen. We have to do this together because mental health is created socially.

You're not just a parent, a caregiver, or an educator. You're a culture maker.

Are you ready? There's a lot at stake here! Let's begin.

Chapter One
Mental Illness Affects Us All

AS I MENTIONED IN THE INTRODUCTION, THERE IS NO SUCH THING AS "THOSE PEOPLE." Those who are struggling with mental illness are often those whom we least expect.

Just a few months ago, my friend shared the tragic news of someone they knew who ended their life. This person did all the "right" things according to our culture. They had a good-paying job, went to yoga, exercised daily, ate well, and came from a good home. Why was this their end?

Because our culture loves band-aid solutions.

If medication solved *all* our problems, we wouldn't see mass amounts of people still struggling with anxiety and depression. And if it were just as simple as taking gluten out of our diet, then we would be seeing significant change. But we're not, are we? I call nutrition, mindfulness, self-care jargon, medication, and even counselling the "twenty percent." We base mental health solutions around these things, but let me tell you, if yoga is the answer, we wouldn't still be in a mental health crisis. If mindfulness truly was the solution, suicide rates among teens and adults would be decreasing—not escalating.

Let me give this example that brings it home. If someone wants to lose weight, they often think of working out more. Of course, exercise is beneficial; however, it's just twenty percent of the equation. Experts say that eighty percent of our weight loss success comes from what we put inside us. What we eat is what really matters.

It's no different from healing mental illness. This book is about the eight percent that we have to get right first and then add the other twenty percent. You can't expect clinical answers alone to solve a mental problem. Our brain is healed through human touch.

When I present the content of this book in my parenting seminar, it frustrates me to no end when parents ask, "But what about mindfulness techniques?" "Should I take my child off gluten?"

Wake up, friends! If it was working, it would have worked already. I'm not saying I don't believe in the twenty percent; however, I am saying we need to get the *foundation* in order first, then the twenty percent will benefit us greatly.

This book is about the eighty percent we don't hear about. This book is about the hard foundation we need to build in our lives and homes that will make all the difference.

The eighty percent isn't "sexy." It's not a quick fix. It's the road less travelled—and it's *hard*, often painful. There aren't many who have been willing to take it, which explains society's increasing mental health crisis. But you're different, I know it. You're brave and willing to dive into the grit.

What can help us along our journey is a good dose of empathy. As a culture, we are patient and understanding about physical illness, but we lose our sense of connected humanity when someone struggles with a mental illness. This is most likely because physical illness is easier to observe. Mental struggles can appear like laziness, rebellion, or weakness. It's hard to have compassion for someone we believe is too sensitive or entitled. The irony is that our judgments only sink them further into their mental prison while confirming to us the story we have determined about them, which only spirals them down further into their rabbit hole. It's a vicious cycle.

In my line of work, I see daily the effects of mental illness. How many teachers have confessed to me over coffee they can't continue in their line of work because of burnout and not being able to handle the pain another student committing suicide? How many youths have shown me the scars on their arms from numbing the pain of their lives through a blade?

Far too many.

A teacher recently emailed me, "As a mom and educator, there are too many young people dying because of lack of supports and understanding. I spent yesterday in the ER with yet another student who attempted suicide. Two funerals in eight months and so many visits to the hospital for my daughter and her best friend."

A student once said to me, "My goal this semester is to get through the year alive."

Online bullying looks like messages in your inbox that say things like, "Why don't you just go kill yourself already?" Students throw the word "suicide" around like it's casual. Instead of saying, "I'm having a rough day," they say, "Ugh, I just want to kill myself." Students have said to me that when someone tries to tell someone else that they are suicidal, the response is usually, "Get in line. So is everyone else" or, "They're just looking for attention."

I often tell youth in my assembly talks that they could literally save someone's life by adopting new language that doesn't use "suicide" or "suicidal" to express a rough day. That way, they know when someone says something, they need to take it seriously. And to those who think those who use suicide threats as a means of getting attention? Honestly, if someone is that desperate, then it's a cry for help. They honestly *do* need the attention.

It's looking a little *Lord of the Flies* out there, folks.

Where are on earth are the adults?!

We've exited the building.

In a recent theatre show I produced, one of the artists, Zoe Slusar, tackled suicide in her piece. Listen to the power in her spoken word: "If I could choose something as powerful as death, then I realized I also could choose something as powerful as life." More than ever, youth need to hear that there's hope. They need the adults back on the playing field with them, guiding, leading, and supporting.

There are repercussions when peers, over parents, become the primary nurturers of each other. Because when that happens, it's *Lord of the* (freakin') *Flies*.

From the moment our children are born, we're constantly being told to get them as far away from us as possible. Sleep training so they can sleep through the night without you. Reading articles on "How to get your preschooler to detach from you in order to go to preschool." We're dumping our children off at every program and camp we can so they can learn their independence and we can have a break. We can't wait to send them back to school, where we expect the teacher to instil education and values into our children so that we don't have to. In mom's groups, moms compare whose child is able to do the most things independently.

We don't push our kids away from us because we don't care about our kids; rather, we do this because our culture has "sold" this to us.

I'm calling all the adults back to the game. Let's get off our phones, let's re-evaluate the world we are letting our kids live in, and let's lead and nurture them. I'm calling us to courage. I'm asking us to stop listening to shame that tells us how awful we're doing as parents, which only keeps us with our head buried in the sand while our children suffer. While reading this book, you may hear shame's voice whisper in your ear. Guess what? I want you to tell shame to "Shove it!"

You're not a bad parent.

No matter how bleak your situation looks, there's hope, and you can create it for your family.

There's no such thing as a perfect parent.

Will you rise above shame?

Will you put on courage instead?

Even a shaky "yes" will do. Let's go get our kids back from the mental prisons that hold them.

Chapter Two
Our Story

MY HUSBAND AND I WERE THRILLED WHEN OUR FIRST SON WAS BORN. WE'D BEEN GREATLY anticipating having a baby, and welcomed him home on a warm September day.

However, this joyous parenting dream was soon shattered—or at least altered. As our son grew from an infant to a toddler, we had a hunch something was off… either that, or this parenting gig was flippin' harder than we thought! My son was defiant from a young age. He wouldn't listen, he'd throw tantrums, he wanted his way, and was just plain hard to manage. Sounds like a typical toddler, right? We thought the stage would outgrow itself.

But it didn't.

He continued like this into kindergarten. We had to make plans around our son's moods. He couldn't seem to do simple tasks, like putting on his shoes when asked. The scenario would go something like this:

"Son, it's time to go. Go get your shoes on."

Nothing.

"Son, it's time to go! Please, go get your shoes on."

Nothing.

"Son, it's time to go! Please, go get your SHOES ON NOW."

Nothing.

And repeat.

At this point, I would be about to lose my mind. *What is wrong with this kid?!* I'd think. *Now we're running late, and I've been more than patient. Okay, one last time…*

"GO. GET. YOUR. SHOES. ON. NOW!"

Still nothing.

It would now be about the ninth time and I'd be at the point of yelling.

My son would look at me as if to ask, "What's wrong with Mom?"

Tenth time, and I'd be using "colourful" language (which is probably how my son learned to curse).

My son was clearly distressed, but *still* not getting his bloody shoes on!

Out of desperation and sheer anger, I'd resort to name-calling and—sigh— the damage was done. The words came out. I couldn't take them back. My poor son would be crying *and* we'd be officially late for wherever we were going. This would happen a couple of times a day. It was exhausting.

In his defiance, there were times when he simply refused to budge. Summer holidays were a nightmare. He was just plain miserable, and he made sure we were, too. There were times when I had to bring my neighbour over to reason with him because he would stand his ground and refuse to do anything I said. His opposition ruled our home and caused us much distress. My background in child development told me this was a little over the top, but I had never been a parent. *Maybe this is what parenting is like? How do parents make this look so easy?* I wondered, tormented.

Then our second son was born, and as he grew into a toddler, we saw an enormous difference. There were still tantrums, but it wasn't anything like we experienced with our oldest. We were exhausted from barely sleeping for four years, having a young one, and raising a child whose behaviour was going to send us to the looney bin. We knew we needed an assessment for answers.

When we were told there was a two-year waiting list, there was no way we were going to wait that long. We were so desperate for answers, we took $5,000 out of our pension and paid for an assessment, which was extremely thorough. (When you pay $5,000, you receive great service.) The assessment came back and it confirmed what we were sensing:

- Anxiety
- Depression
- Oppositional Defiance Disorder
- ADHD

We finally had answers. We could finally move on with our lives. But wait. Now what? Yes, we had answers, and we knew what we were dealing with, but we had no idea how to help our son. We had answers, but we were left with needing so many more.

We had spent all our money on the assessment and didn't have any left over to pay for counselling. We were left on our own to get our son the help he needed. We went from pediatrician to doctor to psychiatrist, only to have the doors slam in front of us. We would wait for months for an appointment, only to find out they couldn't help us.

"We don't see a problem with your son." *That's because he acted like an angel the entire appointment!*

"Look at his assessment. Are you not listening to what we said about what just happened in our home today?"

"We don't think his diagnosis is severe enough to do anything at this point. Come back in a year if he hasn't improved."

A year? You want me to continue to live in this chaos for another year? I need help now! It was beyond frustrating.

We had our answers; still, nothing changed. Depression for our son didn't show up as sadness. Rather, it showed up as severe aggression, destroying our home, yelling, swearing, and punching. Our days were filled with outbursts of anger and tears of frustration from all sides.

It all hit the fan when my son turned eight years old and started mentioning he wanted to *end his life*. From time to time, he would also mention an urge he had to hurt us, too. This was not only shocking, but also disturbing, to hear.

During one appointment, the psychiatrist said, "We can't help your son unless he shows us signs of being in distress." *Here we are again*, I thought. As I told her about his suicide statements, she mentioned to me that the next time he threatened suicide, I had to take him to the hospital. Okay, so that was our plan. We knew what we needed to do next time.

But we had no idea how much that would send our life spinning.

The next time our son threatened suicide, he was in a downward spiral of an enormous outburst. My husband and I managed to get him in our vehicle. We checked into the local children's hospital and waited overnight in a small room, not even knowing what we were waiting for. All I knew was that this is where the psychiatrist told us to go. My son was also confused; he moved from freaking out to fear.

"Why am I here, Mommy?!"

"We're going to get you the help you need," was all I could think of to say.

The next morning, we were able to see a doctor, who then assessed our situation. After what seemed like forever, our son was admitted to the Children's Hospital Mental Health Unit for an indefinite stay.

I didn't expect this.

"You mean to say my son is going to stay here *indefinitely*?"

I wasn't allowed to stay with him. He was led to a room that he would be sharing with another boy just a few years older. I looked at my son's eyes filled with fear as I was escorted out of the unit. I tried to be brave, but broke down into sobs once I left. I promised my son we would visit every chance we were allowed.

Did I make the right decision? Is this really going to help?

I felt lost, like I just handed my child over to who-knows-what. Would they take good care of him? Would he feel lonely? Was he scared? I've never felt more out of control in my life.

We visited him every day for two hours in the afternoon and two hours in the evening. This threw our life upside down. We had to figure out childcare for our youngest. We took a lot of time off work. Every goodbye was painful, watching my son's fear, wondering why we would do this to him.

He was only eight. How could he possibly understand why we would do this? I questioned this every day, as well. How could I not? It was heartbreaking to see the children in the mental health unit. One boy was only six.

We were able to have regular appointments with the family psychologist at the hospital. During our first appointment, the psychologist asked, "So what do you do when your son throws his fits of rage?" I told her I would send him to his room and that he would be able to come out when he was ready to be a "good boy." I waited for her praise of my excellent parenting, only to be surprised by her response.

What she said changed everything. *Everything.*

She replied, "Oh no, you *never* send the hurting away from you. You bring them *closer.*"

I was confused. At first, I thought that sounded ridiculous. Bring my son "closer," when he's wrecking our house and hurling profanities at me? That sounded like letting him get away with his horrible behaviour. What would it even look like to "bring him closer"? I never pictured him as "hurting," only acting out. I saw my son as rebellious needing to be disciplined. This concept was foreign to me.

After three weeks of hospitalization, my son was discharged. After three years of crying out for help, we now had a psychiatrist, a counsellor, and medication that seemed to be working for him. I was thrilled to get home and move on with a son who was now, for all intents and purposes, "fixed."

Was I ever wrong! The hardest part of our journey was yet to come.

Chapter Three
Bring Them Closer?

THE FIRST WEEK HOME FROM THE HOSPITAL WAS JOYOUS. MY SON WAS SO HAPPY TO BE back home. He seemed like a new kid! Whatever medication they had him on were like miracle pills. I relaxed into what I believed was our "new normal."

And then… the rage started up again. I'll never forget the despair I felt when that first episode after the hospital occurred.

Is this what our life is going to be like forever? All that time in the hospital for what? Nothing! If that didn't help, what will?

I was just about to send him to his room when I remembered the psychologist's words: "Bring him closer."

I still didn't know what that meant, but for this particular episode of rage, I kept him with me. I removed all the knives and sharp objects. I tried to put my arms around him, but he pushed me away. I didn't know what to do.

I said to him, through tears, "Son, we love you. You belong in our home. We're going to do whatever it takes to help you. Nothing is more important than our connection with you."

My son was suspicious; after all, he was used to being sent to his room, to being yelled at. This new "method" threw him off, and he wasn't having it. He didn't trust me. He thought this was just another way to get him to "behave." He acted worse just to test if I really meant what I was saying. It was hard—really hard—keeping him in the same room.

It's difficult to work through your own emotions when someone is completely losing it around you—especially when they know what buttons to push. My son knew just the right insults to hurl at me that would make me blow. Some days I lost it. Other days I kept it together. The important thing is that I kept showing up the same way, time after time. I kept showing up. And then I showed up some more. I showed up consistently the same way for an entire year.

I stayed with him in his distress. I took the insults, the screaming, the swearing, etc., always reassuring him, "Son, my connection to you is more important right now than changing your behaviour." He would yell more, swear more, get in my face all the more to prove his theory that this was all just BS.

But it wasn't. I meant it—as much as this went directly against everything I knew about parenting and discipline. I imagined my dad rolling over in his grave, telling me to "Stop being such a hippie and discipline that boy! What he needs is for you to smack that rebellion out of him."

Eventually, my son began to trust me, allowing me to hold him whenever his big emotions were exploding out of him. Now, all it takes is for me to put my arm around him saying, "We got you," and he softens.

That year was one of the hardest years of my life because while I had to be strong to hold a safe space for my son, it felt like all my unresolved issues came bubbling to the surface. As I held my son, I didn't know if I could hold my own emotions. I would hold it all in, only to explode later or burst into tears behind closed doors. Other times, we both lost it at the same time.

I couldn't handle his extreme emotions—that's why I used to send him to his room; it was honestly a lot easier. I wish I could have seen glimmers of hope during that season. I wish I could have had a sense that all the pain would be worth it. Some days, I fell into such deep despair because I thought this was what life was going to be like forever. I didn't know if bringing my son "closer" in his pain was even working.

I was angry at anyone I could potentially blame for this. My husband was the first place I started. "If it weren't for your issues…" When I couldn't blame him any longer, I blamed the school system, then the mental health care system, then God… but it didn't help. The "blame game" was getting me nowhere, except closer to bitterness as I wondered what I did to deserve this lot in life. I've never felt more out of control, more powerless, more lonely than I did in that season.

I lost friends because I could rarely go out since my husband was unable to emotionally handle our son's outbursts. Extended family wanted to help, but honestly didn't know how to handle him. Sometimes sending him to their homes only made things worse, because they would lose their cool out of their frustration, spiralling my son further downward. We couldn't get babysitters because my son threw a fit if we left him with someone else.

We were shut in, isolated, and often misunderstood by others—including some of our closest friends. Eventually, my son's anxiety at school grew so extreme that I had to remove him from school in the spring to homeschool him. Now, on top of everything else, I couldn't work.

It was the loneliest time of my life. It's true when they say no one brings casseroles when someone's struggling with mental illness. However, as the year progressed, so did my son's health. It increased significantly when I brought him home from school in the spring. He slept most of the first week. He was exhausted from having to hide his anxiety to put on a brave face each day. I can't imagine doing that in Grade Four. How hard that must have been on his mind and body.

I noticed his episodes lessened the more I worked on becoming emotionally regulated myself. We began to connect—and even laugh—at times. There was a light at the end of the tunnel.

As I write this book, my son is twelve years old. You would never guess his mental health history. No one would know because he's living a normal life now. He still has big emotions at times, but we now know how to work with him to see him regulate and feel secure. He is going through normal adjustments to adolescence—which honestly feels like a cakewalk compared to where we've been.

My son's journey back to health made me realize that we are putting up with far too much regarding the mental health crisis our children are facing. When one or two children here and there struggle mentally, that's one thing, but when it seems an entire generation is in crisis, we—the adults—need to wake up.

I believe most of us have come to accept that "this is just the way it is." I'm here to say it is *not* the way it has to be! My son's story can be the story of others as well. Society's issues are only there as long as we decide to put up with them. I say "Enough!" to anxiety, depression, and suicide tormenting our children. It's time for the adults to rise up and take back our kids!

This book is going to tell you how to do that. I'll be sharing everything I did to bring my son from suicidal and oppositional to connected to us and whole again. I'm going to be real and frank, because I'm not messing around. I want nothing but wholeness for your children and your family.

I will leave this chapter with a note I wrote to my son during that first month home after the hospital. I put this in a frame in his room so he would always see it:

Home is a safe place
We are allowed to make mistakes
You can be yourself
We care about you
We will not allow anything to be
more important than our connection with you
Your obedience,
your respect level,
and your success
will not be more important
than our connection with you

Looking back, I realize I probably wrote that for me just as much as I did for him, to remind me that I was in this for the long haul, for his benefit only, and for me to be willing to surrender my agenda and desired outcomes.

Are you ready to see healing for your family? This is going to take more courage and grit you never knew you had, but I promise you that you have it.

Now it's time to rewrite *your* story.

Chapter Four
Shame and Parenting

I COULD WRITE AN ENTIRE BOOK ON MY EPIC PARENTING FAILS.

Before we move further, I want to clarify that the intention of this book is not to tell you about everything you're doing wrong and what you should be doing instead. We get enough of that already. From messages in the media, to books that remind us how much we "suck" and will never measure up, to other parents giving us "the stink eye"… Please know that this book is officially a shame-free zone.

When my youngest son was four, he had an electric guitar from Fisher-Price he adored. It was his favourite. He was a destructive child, and would often accidentally break my things. One day, he broke something special of mine and I just lost it. I took his precious guitar, smashed it on the floor. "This is how it feels to have something you love broken!" I yelled.

My intention was to teach him empathy for how others feel when something they love is broken, but this clearly failed as I looked up into his devastated eyes. He was crushed. Even a few years later, while looking through his memory book, he noticed a picture of the guitar and began crying. "Mommy, why would you do such a thing?!"

Epic Parenting Fail. Shame had a hay day with me on that one.

During one of my oldest son's counselling sessions, the counsellor brought up bravery. "I'm not brave; I'm a coward," my son proclaimed. This broke my heart because all I saw—and *see*—in him is bravery. At that time in his life, he was so incredibly anxious. We could hardly get him to leave the house, even to go over to his friend's. Every time he would leave the house, he was choosing bravery, even though he would never see it that way.

How many of us have thought the same? "I'm not brave; I'm a coward." Yet every day you wake up to face another day, you are *brave*. Every time you want to run and hide but you stay put, you are *brave*. For every moment you love your family instead of packing your bags, you are *brave*. Each time you leave the house when all you want to do is isolate, you are *brave*. For every time you love when you've been hurt, you are *brave*.

You are braver than you think.

I'll never forget this one time I was teaching movement at a school. I always teach in a circle, and, at times, invite students to find their courage by dancing in the middle. A girl who had experienced a brain injury entered into the middle of the circle to dance. I didn't think much of it until the teachers explained to me that she hadn't been able to move very well up until that day. She was tormented daily by anxiety, so for her to enter the circle was nothing short of a miracle. The teachers were blown away.

I think of that girl every time I feel I'm facing something I can't overcome. The truth is, there's nothing we can't overcome. There's no situation too impossible where hope is out of reach.

While you read this book, you might be triggered to remember all your epic parenting fails. At that moment, I want you to tell shame to "shove it" and remember you are *brave*. Rarely will you feel courageous, but be courageous anyway! Look at how much is inside of you. Many of us have lost our true selves in the storms of life.

Courage starts with: "I am enough."

With that as our foundation, let's get into it.

Chapter Five

What's the Real Problem?

THE MENTAL HEALTH CRISIS IS EVERYWHERE WE LOOK. INCREASED RATES OF SUICIDE, bullying, self-harm. I see it right in front of me in schools where I do my resilience work. The second leading cause of death among young people today is suicide. One out of every five students struggles with a mental health issue and everyone is trying to peg the culprit of responsibility.

"It's those screens, I tell you."

"It's violent video games."

"It's food-related."

"It's because of pop culture."

"We are too isolated. There's no extended family to help. We don't know our neighbours."

"The cost of living today is ridiculous. We work endless hours for little pay *and* have to pay for daycare on top of it all. There's no time for family."

Everyone has an opinion of what they believe is the number-one reason we're all suffering. To be honest, *all* of the above are contributing factors. Screens, such as smartphones and iPads, have made their debut only in the last ten years. There are only preliminary studies on how this has affected children born from 2005 to now. The way we produce our food has changed. Pop culture and today's video games equal junk values with side-effects no different from junk food overconsumption. We are more isolated than ever.

Growing up, I always had adults who spoke encouragement to me. My neighbours always knew where I was and what I was doing (and had no problem telling my parents when I was up to no good). My grandparents were my caregivers when my parents were working. There were more "Coach Carters," such as youth leaders, teachers, and coaches who went beyond the call of duty to invest in the youth they were leading.

Today, adults and educators are burned out from being overworked, and red tape that restricts their potential to invest in youth. Today, we don't have family to look after our kids, and yet the need for both parents to work has never been greater. But it goes so much further than that. While we're all looking to pin down the "one thing" to blame, the real culprit is hiding among us.

If it's not specifically video games, screens, or isolation, then what is it? I have found that the real problem is… *me*. I played the "blame game" for years, trying to pin the problem onto a person or a system, or screens, but it was all futile. It all led back to me staring at myself in the mirror, seeing my own emotional dysregulation, my own brokenness, my own inability to cope with my anxiety.

The truth is, I didn't realize I hadn't made sense of my own story. I wasn't aware of how much was buried inside of me from the past, and how it was affecting my parenting. Why was I so angry? Why would I yell? I'm not an angry person. I don't yell at people on a regular basis. I didn't realize that not making sense of my story was not allowing me to connect with my children the way I wanted to.

I began to get curious about why I would become so angry and yell. I stopped judging myself and told shame to "shove it" so I could really notice what was happening. I began to recall all the times as a child I didn't feel heard or understood. I was a chatterbox, a verbal processor. I would talk my parents' ears off! I would notice when they started to tune me out, and it hurt. I was also a very emotional child. My dad didn't "do emotions." If I was sad, I was told to tone it down and stop crying. Anger was not acceptable—neither was being overly excited. I was an emotional volcano waiting to erupt.

Then I married someone who also couldn't handle my emotions or my need to explain every thought and idea I had. I felt that no one understood me, or wanted to hear me. My parents, my husband didn't hear me—so when I had children, I thought *they* would listen to me. They would understand me.

You can see where this is going, can't you? For me, to put that kind of expectation on my children was not only unrealistic, but also damaging. Children aren't going to listen because, guess what? They're just kids. I began to notice that my anger was not actually directed at my children, but rather directed at all the times I didn't feel heard. As soon as I made sense of my story, I was able to get a grip on my anger and yelling. Now I don't lose it like I used to.

Making sense of our story helps us to name what's really going on, instead of reading articles like, "Three ways to stop yelling at your child," only to find us right back at the same place again. Why? Because we don't need tools and systems. This isn't an outward problem; it's an inward one.

Your issue isn't that you yell; there's something *underneath*.

Your problem isn't anger; there's a bigger story at play.

Our job is to discover what it is.

This will take courage because it's the harder road. It's so much easier to apply those "Three simple strategies to stop yelling." The problem is that the root is still there. You'll only find yourself back at the same place again and again, with shame increasing each time.

Being on the other side of crisis and looking back I see that:

The person who changed the most in our family was me.

The person who had to do the most internal work was me.

This took more courage and vulnerability than I knew I had because everything in my upbringing taught me that parents are always right. Parents never get it wrong.

I am homesick for a place I'm not even sure exists. One where my heart is full, my body is loved, and my soul understood. (Melissa Cox, source unknown)

Too many of us parents feel homesick. We don't feel understood, we don't feel we belong, and neither do our kids. How are we supposed to create belonging in our homes when we don't feel like we belong? We can give only what we have. Belonging is one of those things that doesn't come cheap. You can only give it away if you own it yourself—deep down.

This is where many of us need to start. We need to make sense of our story so we can begin to write better stories for our children.

Chapter Six
Putting Our Significance in the Hands of Others

LET'S GET DOWN TO ONE OF THE ROOTS OF OUR STRUGGLE.

Today's culture celebrates significance. One of our greatest mistakes as humans is to think our significance comes from others: being around the "right" people, receiving affirmation, needing to be seen as someone important. Being the perfect parent or having a struggle-free marriage.

We need to get real. We need to let go of unrealistic expectations. We need to lay down our need to be important. What if you lived like you already had significance?

What would be different for you?

There will always be critics. We pay way too much attention to them. A while ago, I formed a small list of people whose opinion matters most to me. It was a list of people who love me, even in my weakness, and whom I know have my best interest in mind. Only the ones on my list are allowed to speak constructive criticism into my life, because I trust them not to tell me what I *want* to hear, but rather what I *need* to hear. This keeps me grounded in my identity and allows me to continue to be brave and to risk. I know that if I'm out of line, my friends will redirect me. Most of all, it keeps me from focusing on those who just don't understand me.

We pay far too much attention to those who don't understand us. We tell ourselves stories in our minds that are often fabricated and blown out of proportion. Heart wounds happen when what we want to believe about ourselves goes against the negative labels others impose on us. Often, those "others" are the ones closest to us, such as parents, partners, and friends whom we assumed would have our backs.

People reveal our heart wounds. A heart wound makes it so that instead of speaking life to someone else, we speak from our woundedness. Heart wounds distort our perception and cloud our vision to see things the way they really are. This results in misreading situations and not understanding what people are really trying to communicate. Heart wounds happen when what we believe about ourselves and what others impose on us is different. We don't know how to navigate this tension. We either push people away, putting up a fortress around our heart, or we allow people to walk all over us, only to later make us resent them.

Heart wounds come from implicit memories—the ones buried deep inside that form patterns of thought and behaviours that we don't even notice. Implicit memories are formed by people and experiences in your life. The truth is, you're constantly having a narrative imposed on you by others. Years of your family's lineage has written on you a code of genetics, forming the construction of who you are. "Genetics" is just a fancy scientific term that describes the story that has been designed for you by your family history. You are a thread in a greater tapestry created for you.

People were telling your story before you were born. Your parents spoke of how excited they were to be having a baby, or your mother was petrified because she wasn't expecting you. The caregivers whom you were going to meet when you came into the world were talking about what your name would be, where you would be living. Some had a room ready for you, beautifully decorated to say, "Welcome to our home." Others made plans to find you a home that would be better suited for you. And others, unfortunately, allowed you to enter into a world of violence and chaos.

People continued to tell your story while you were a baby: "What a cutie!" "Wow, that baby is fat!" "Does she ever stop crying?" "What a colicky baby."

And as a toddler: "Don't mind her; she's just shy." "He's my little monkey, always getting into mischief."

As you entered school, your story continued to be written by teachers and peers. You found out you were a "good student" or a "bad student." You found out if you were "cool" or a "loser." The friend group you were placed in determined how you identified yourself. At home, you were either encouraged or considered a "nuisance."

People are constantly speaking words of identity over you.

When I was in middle school, I was called "Connie Chunk" because I was the "big girl" in school. I took on this label and let it define me through middle school, high school, and college. I was the bubbly fat girl. I believed that's all I was. I was the girl whom the boys would become friends with because I was "safe"—they wouldn't fall for me. They would tell me all their secret crushes while I crushed on them. I believed I didn't deserve to be loved. I was charismatic and funny to cover up my insecurity.

At twenty-two years old, I joined a hip-hop class to lose weight. I loved it— that is, until the end of the class when we formed a circle in the middle of which everyone had to take a turn dancing. The last place you want to be when you've taken on a negative label is in the middle of a circle. You don't want to be seen, yet, at the same time, you so desperately want to be seen.

I entered the circle hesitantly, danced the dorkiest move ever, and told myself I'd never go back to that class. But then a girl next to me in the circle said, "Wow! You are so courageous!" I was taken aback. She didn't see the "fat girl?"

Something changed in my mind that day simply because someone spoke something different. I chose to take on this new label of "courageous" and went back to class each week. I went for over a year and began teaching the youth I was working with all my moves. I discovered hip hop connected with at-risk youth and opened my own hip-hop studio where we invested in their lives through this urban art form. I would have never done this unless someone offered me a new story I could choose to accept.

Not too long ago, I found all my old elementary report cards. I didn't realize, even as early as Grade One, I was behind in reading, math, comprehension, and basic tasks. In school, I was a compliant student, but not "smart" in an academic sense. This was always the case, from elementary, through high school, to college. I found out only recently that all this time, I've had ADHD. As my kids laughed at my marks and the teachers' comments in the report cards, I was able to encourage them that even though we may have challenges, it doesn't ever stop us from living the purpose for which we were born.

Perhaps I didn't quite measure up academically, but I've owned two companies, overseen two non-profit organizations, authored three books, produced six theatre productions, led numerous teams, and have spoken to audiences from all over for the past two decades.

Don't let anything or anyone ever tell you that you're limited.

We choose to either reject or accept the stories others impose on us. To reject disempowering stories takes an incredible amount of resilience that most of us don't have. The reason others affect you so much isn't that you're weak; rather, it's that the mirror neurons you have in your brain. What's making this hard for you isn't your lack of self-esteem, but neuroscience.

Science tells us that, as humans, we can't help but want to connect with others and "mirror" them, especially those whom we call family. When a mother looks into the eyes of her baby and smiles, that baby lights right up! That concept doesn't change, whether we're babies, forty years old, or eighty years old. People affect us because of this interpersonal neurobiology at play. Your brain is wired to want to connect with others. This is why their opinion matters to you. This is why the story that others speak over you hold so much power. The good news is that you can rise above these stories others have imposed upon you.

One thing I've learned is that if you're looking for rejection, you'll have no problem finding it. You need to learn how to keep moving—even when there's no affirmation from others. Keep being courageous, even when there's no inspiring music behind you. People don't owe you loyalty. If that's what you want from people, you'll just end up disappointed. Desiring people to be loyal to you, and keeping a record of who isn't, is toxic behaviour.

Most mothers admit their source of shame comes from other mothers. People everywhere feel pressured to live that perfect Instagram life full of filters so the people around us see only our best side. Can't we see how much damage this is doing to our sense of connection to ourselves and others? Being overly concerned with how you appear to others imprisons both you and them.

Do you ever find yourself wondering exactly where you "fit?" There are times when I feel I fit in and can move around my environment in comfort. But other times, I feel intimidated and shrink back in fear.

Ever feel like that?

Not too long ago, I was participating in a kickboxing class and the instructor had us line up along each wall, then walk to the middle of the gym. Whoever was directly in front of us was our partner. I was right in the middle of my row. I walked to the middle of the gym only to find that somehow, the waters had parted. Everyone had a partner—except *me*. How did that happen? I got stuck with the instructor who kicked my butt.

A woman came up to me after and said, "Don't take it personally if no one wants to be your partner in this class. It's not you; it's because you're short, and they're all tall and naturally like to partner with other tall people."

Huh? Was that supposed to make me feel better? It's amazing how in those moments, you're rushed right back to junior high with those same feelings of insecurity.

Whatever our past was like, it can still affect us in our adult life, even though we think it shouldn't.

Not only was I "Connie Chunk" in school, but I also felt like an ugly duckling. I had massive buck teeth that stuck out of my mouth. In Grade Eight, I got braces—so, silver buck teeth. I longed to be one of the pretty girls who seemed to have endless amounts of friends and admiration. I went through all junior and senior high feeling overlooked. Even twenty years since high school, the insecurity is still there, trying to control my every move. So here we are, still trying to constantly find where we fit. It's still Grade Eight, just more "adult-looking."

Stop trying to fit in. Could it be that we were never meant to fit anywhere? Could it be that we waste a significant amount of time trying to find ourselves in the "right" circle of friends or in the "perfect" job?

The fact is, when we stop trying to fit in, we can find our place and our voice. We find this is where we make the best contribution to others and society. If everyone was like you or me, nothing would happen—just a lot of the same. When you step out of just choosing to "fit in," you'll ruffle some feathers. Some might not like it, because you're "disturbing the peace." Are you okay with that? You'll need to toughen up a little bit and let a whole load of useless opinions roll off your back. I'm calling you out of the mundane into something significant—something that affects not just today or tomorrow, but generations to come.

Don't make yourself small just to fit. It's time to not fit in. It's time to find your unique voice. It's time to do what you do best. It's time for you to think about what impact you make when you're *not* fitting in. Do you dare?

What would you do if you weren't intimidated? Is that scary thought? Very! Is it lonely? Sometimes. Does it feel vulnerable? Yes. Don't be afraid of resistance. Nothing develops depth and capacity in our lives more than resistance. We must let go of striving on our own and surrender to its purpose in our lives. The beauty it brings is worth it because it empties us of ourselves and brings what may have looked desirable to its true light. Success is different from purpose. Being around the "right" people is empty. Find beauty in things you love and that love you back. The temptation in today's culture is to *look* good without actually *being* good.

"Recall the feeling you have when someone praises you, when you are approved, applauded and accepted and when you succeeded. Contrast that with the kind of feeling you get when you really enjoy what you do and enjoy the good company you do it with. One is a feeling of self glorification, the other of self fulfillment. Feelings of self promotion or self glorification were invented by your society to make you productive and controllable. They were meant to produce thrills, excitement, and emptiness." (Anthony De Mello, source unknown)

Self-criticism is death. Self-esteem is not how good you feel about yourself; rather, it's the independence you choose to have from the evaluations you impose on yourself and the from the judgments of others. If you don't enjoy yourself, you'll end up rejecting yourself and offer this "rejected self" to the world around you. Remind yourself you don't have to do what everyone else is doing.

The other day, my youngest was having a rough day, so I took him by the arms, held him up, and had him look me in the eyes. "Stand tall. You are loved," I said. As soon as I said that, his head dropped. This reminded me of how much we *all* need to hear, "Stand tall. You are loved."

Where do you find your belonging? Some find their belonging in family or friends; others find their belonging in their work. The problem with finding your belonging in someone or something you do is that you will often find disappointment. We need to find belonging in *ourselves*.

Even this can disappoint, because I'm often my own worst critic. In my experience, the belonging I create for myself comes with more conditions than others tend to put on me. I'll never forget the day when I just realized I belong. I can't explain it. It just became real to me. I always "knew" I belonged in my mind, but on this day, it became grounded deep in my heart. We all "know" we belong. We know we deserve to be here on earth and have a place, but have you ever experienced just knowing you belong deep in your gut?

This happened to me one morning while having my morning coffee and quiet time with God. It came to me like a revelation. Suddenly, no one could convince me otherwise. I belong because I belong to someone, something far greater than myself. What if I was created for a purpose? What if my life was created not by me, not by others, but created? What if I was known by this Creator? It hit me that my belonging was found in the One who created me. This kind of belonging could never be stolen from me because it doesn't come from a person or something fleeting. It didn't depend on me to create it for myself, which honestly has always felt like such pressure.

Then it hit me—if I belong to something so incredible, then I can extend my hand of belonging to anyone because no person creates belonging for me. I could extend belonging to those who have misjudged me, rejected me. I could extend my hand of belonging, even to an enemy, because my belonging is a gift I receive that I can give to others.

I can extend it to my husband when he hurts me. I can offer it to my children when they are unthankful for all I do for them. I have a heart tattoo now on my right wrist that reminds me of the day this became real to me. The heart points outwards to remind me "all are welcome in my presence because I am welcome." The tattoo forever reminds me of this day that changed everything for me.

Are you wondering what on earth this all has to do with parenting?

Everything.

Who you are, your beliefs about yourself, and the story others have imposed on you, the story you have chosen to believe about yourself all affect every single relationship you have. Your marriage, your friendships, your colleagues, and the relationship you have with your children.

Think about it. That recent time you yelled at your spouse—was that really about them, or were you responding to a past memory that has affected your present argument? Could the way you interact with your children be different if you made sense of your story and where memories have affected the way you view the scenarios you face with them each day? Would your friendships be more meaningful if you had a better perspective on yourself? Would you stay in your friend group that exists only to gossip and judge others?

I'm calling parents to courage:
• Courage to tell your story.
• Courage to hear others' stories.
• Courage to know our stories can be rewritten.

As you continue reading, I'm calling the courage in you to rise up and to have the same revelation I received—that you *belong*. The story that others have imposed on you doesn't have the final say. Your story, your family's story, is *yours* to write. You can decide today to face the wounds and the heartache, and create for your home something different. There's no abuse, no addiction, no mental illness that can withstand a courageous person with resolve. You have what it takes to make it. You're not alone. You're surrounded by others fighting the same battle. I'm calling us to stand together so that no family is left behind, because the truth is, we can't do this alone.

We need one another.

Courage is contagious. Are you ready to face yourself and your family's story? Read on, brave one. We're only just beginning.

Chapter Seven

Your Family's Future Is Yours to Write

EXPERIENCES SHAPE US AND CREATE OUR STORY.

How you make sense of what happened to you in your childhood and your adult life is crucial. How you make sense of how those experiences have influenced you today is even *more* critical. It's not just our childhood experiences we need to look at, but the experiences that have shaped us throughout our lives.

Death, grief, abusive relationships, toxic work environments all shape us. Making sense of how they affect our day-to-day relationships is important. The connection your child has with you is strongly connected to how you understand your life experiences. If we have not made sense of, or properly processed, our life experiences, this will have a profound impact on how we react to our children and the other relationships in our lives. Our response towards our children and others can then become over-the-top emotional reactions and impulsive behaviours.

We wonder why parenting seems to bring out the worst in us. The great news is that no matter what your experiences have been, they don't have to be the end of your story.

Parents and caregivers have an incredible opportunity to shape children's brains through a safe, empowering environment. This means that if a child is struggling, there is still hope to see their brain moulded through positive experiences.

I used to teach an empathy workshop in a school. I would ask the high school students, "Do you create who you are, or do others create who you are?"

Through a unique method, I take students through a process so that they're able to see how hard it is for someone to become resilient without the help of others around them.

Unfortunately, our world doesn't make this easy. We're often told we create ourselves and our own destiny. The only person in control of whether you reach your goals and live to your full potential is *you*. No one does it for you. But we make it harder for people to do that when we mistreat them, abuse them, and put them down. Studies of the results of trauma prove this. And despite our desire to be authentic, we live in a world where we learn how to show up. Showing authenticity for many is social—and even professional—suicide. For youth in school, they learn what masks and armour to put on so they aren't judged.

Our assumptions and judgments of others keep their armour on, making us feel justified in our assumptions of them. The bully gets called out instead of seeing the hurting, frightened person underneath. The shy girl is labelled a snob. The oppositional child is called rebellious. We humans have the ability to take one another's armour off to see the person for who they really are. It takes an incredible amount of vulnerability to see past the exterior of another person and find the gold inside of them, but when we do, people become beautiful—even those who seem to be the hardest to love. We have a responsibility to build one another up, speak destiny over them, and not tear them down.

Who created you? What experiences, people, and situations have shaped the person who stands here today? Who are you *without* your pain? The person you are without your pain is the person you really are. It peels back all the layers of negative experiences and reveals that small child inside of you who loves freely—who's full of life and curiosity. It's unresolved trauma that blocks our ability to enjoy meaningful moments with others that keeps us in toxic relationships that only continue to erode us on the inside. It keeps us stuck in survival mode that keeps us from our right to play, imagine, and create.

We view everything through the framework of our own experiences, our family history, and what influences us—what and whom we listen to. I saw a quote that said, "We don't see things the way they are, we see them as the way we are." We get stuck in patterns that don't support who we really want to be. How we perceive situations and experiences determines our response to them. Our early experiences shaped our perception—how we were treated and spoken to. This is why it is important to be mindful of the story we tell ourselves. Often the story we tell ourselves is filled with holes. Some of what we are telling ourselves is true, but there are holes in the story that can be filled only by gaining a perspective outside of ourselves to give the proper context. This is where most misunderstandings, arguments, and divisions come from—not having a full perspective of the whole story.

We live our lives in echo chambers. Algorithms keep us locked into hearing our own voice being echoed back to us. We find our tribe who listens to the same podcasts as we do, reads the same books as we do, believes the same things as we do. We form friendships with people who think just like us. This demonstrates what's happening scientifically in our brains. We can't help but mirror one another as humans. Mirror neurons inside our brains connect us to others. This is why it's hard for us to not have others' moods affect ours. We are literally fighting connection when we resist taking on other people's emotions. Our framework and the "echo chamber" in which we find ourselves also keeps us from understanding what others may feel. It makes it challenging to overcome the stigmas of mental health and trauma. It's the reason our culture is polarized. It's why we are having issues reconciling systemic issues like racism.

The way we perceive directly influences how we behave. The way we perceive comes from how we are treated and communicated to. The mind processes data by creating stories. This is why it's important to notice the story you're telling yourself. It's important as caregivers to make sense of our stories. Behaviour is communication. When we dig under the reason that we might be yelling at our kids, or withdrawing from them, we can remove from ourselves feelings of shame and actually be able to address the underlying issues and become the parents we know we can be.

I entered into parenting with a full emotional suitcase. No parent wants to fail, we just forget to look inside our suitcase and see how some of our baggage is affecting the way we interact with our children.

You might be wondering what I mean by "make sense of your story"… It doesn't necessarily mean going to counsellor after counsellor to dig into the painful details of your childhood. It means becoming curious as to why you respond the way you do in different situations.

Yes, this often means looking into the past, but not always to childhood. Sometimes it takes you back to that moment you lost your job a few years ago and how it has affected you in you didn't even realize. It's going back to moments that have shaped who you are and the way you relate to others today. To make sense of your story means connecting the dots between something that happened to a way you interact with others now. It doesn't necessarily mean making peace with whatever happened, because healing takes time. Making peace with the past is a part of it, but the "making sense" part starts when you have that "eureka!" moment as you see why you react the way you do. It's a starting place.

The way we speak to our children becomes their inner voice. Making sense of our story reveals to us where, why, and how we are triggered. Most of us are surprised when we react harshly towards our children and others. We don't intend to react abruptly, but intentions are very different from actions. We judge ourselves based on our intentions. Others judge us based on what we actually did. The problem with intentions is that they can cloud our own judgment to think we're doing better than perhaps we are. We wonder why our children or partner are complaining about us. Can't they see we're trying? Don't they see the effort we're putting in here? No, they can't. They don't know our intentions; they only know our actions.

It used to drive me nuts when I would bring up an issue with my husband, only to hear him say again and again, "I'm trying!" One time I unkindly responded, "Well, try harder! Your trying isn't good enough." What he was attempting to communicate was that he was having a hard time moving from what he *intended* to do to actually *doing* it. This is something we all struggle with. Moving from intention to action seems so simple, but it's not. It takes an incredible amount of energy, focus, and a commitment to creating new patterns for the long haul.

Our story dictates to us how we respond to our children's behaviour. Those things that drive you crazy may be rooted in your story. Our mind creates patterns that influence the way we perceive behaviours and situations. We want to love our children, but we find ourselves becoming annoyed, frustrated, even angry. Pay attention to what's going on inside of you when your children are driving you bonkers so you can begin to notice how your responses are affecting the relationships and interactions with them.

Not coming to peace with our story disconnects us from our children. It causes impulsive reactions from us that create an unstable, emotional environment in our home. Our children may then become oppositional, anxious, or defensive. When this happens over and over, we create a pattern of disconnection where everyone in the home feels they are on their own, isolated, and no one feels understood.

For the longest time, I couldn't figure out why my son would become unstable when I was disappointed in various situations that didn't involve him. He instantly believed it was his fault. When I asked him about this one day, he replied, "I feel so much shame when you're disappointed, Mom." He was able to explain to me how I would often shame him with my words when he did something wrong. Now any disappointment I felt triggered him. I realized this was a pattern in my life with other relationships, as well. I was great at shaming others, especially my family. I was so proud of my son for bringing up his feelings in a respectful way so I could be brought aware of this pattern and work to change it.

The greatest emotions to pay attention to in yourself is your anger and your sadness. Notice what makes you angry. Dig into why. Often, you'll find the same things that make you angry also make you sad. Anger is often masking sadness; it's an easier emotion to feel. Sadness is a vulnerable feeling. And, of course, notice what makes you happy, as well! Noticing what makes us happy allows us to see the good things we need to cultivate more of in our lives.

I noticed that nothing in life could make me angrier than when my husband would blankly stare at the wall for an hour whenever I brought up issues. As I mentioned earlier, when his only response was, "I'm trying!" I would lose it. After some digging, I realized my anger issues were rooted in me not feeling heard throughout my entire life. Not feeling heard meant I didn't feel valued, which made me feel like I wasn't worth much. When my husband would stare at the wall, the story I told myself was, "I'm not valuable enough to be heard." And when he would respond with, "I'm trying," what I heard was, "You really aren't worth the effort." For all the times I couldn't scream at my parents, I was screaming at my husband. For all the times I couldn't advocate for myself, I was now ready to roar with him. As soon as that made sense to me, I was able to move forward and my husband's responses didn't affect me as much. I was able to be at peace with my husband's own journey.

Our experiences affect how we relate to our children and their story. The way we communicate with our kids affects how they develop. Children learn about themselves by the way we communicate with them. Enjoying your child is vital for your child to have a good self-view. Our nonverbal communication matters even more than our verbal. Facial expressions speak louder than words. An unresolved issue can make us inflexible and unable to choose responses that would be helpful to our children's development. We can find it hard to listen to them because our own internal experiences are being so noisy that it's all we can hear. When we have made sense of our story, we're in control of our responses to our children's behaviour. We're able to choose our response without being controlled by our emotions.

Your story becomes your children's story. We repeat the patterns we learn in childhood. The reason is that we usually repress the hurt we have felt, and don't allow ourselves to feel and process it. We don't realize that packing down hurt creates an emotional whirlwind in our homes where people end up walking on eggshells around us. Our reactions are rarely about the present, but rather about unresolved parts of our story in our past. This only causes confusion to those around us. When we blame, get angry, make excuses, justify ourselves, or lash out, we are protecting ourselves. We don't even realize it. We need to become aware when we are using self-protection methods so we can begin to create new patterns that will increase our connection with those whom we love. We do this by asking ourselves, "What am I really feeling?" "What is my behaviour communicating?" "What part am I playing to create the emotional atmosphere in my home?" etc.

Mental health is created in *connection*. If you think your yoga practice alone is going to guide you to mental wellness, you're going to be disappointed. No meditation, mindfulness, or any individual practice or prescribed medication alone is going to heal us completely. We highly affect one another. You can leave your yoga class feeling at peace only to be met five minutes later by real people in the real world who seem to bring out your worst.

I'm not saying individual steps towards mental health are useless; I'm simply saying that they *alone* aren't the answer. You need others to heal. Connection is the one missing link we have today. The neurobiology of "we" has the potential to heal many issues around anxiety and depression. When I share my story to a kind, attuned friend who listens to me, my brain is rewired—literally! This scientific phenomenon is called "interpersonal neurobiology" and it's greatly untapped in our world. This means that if we can attune to others' stories and experiences, providing safe spaces for them to be heard and understood, they can heal.

But what do we normally do? We tell people to stop overreacting and to "get over it." We instantly jump to try to fix their problem or provide "instant" solutions. We try to help them look on the bright side. We devalue them and their experience by saying things like, "Oh, you think you have problems? Let me tell you about what happened to me…" They leave the conversation feeling unheard, misunderstood, and confused, falling even deeper into the anxiety they felt before.

Telling our own stories, being heard and listening with empathy, can actually bring breakthrough mentally.

When we share our stories and allow others to look into the crevice of our soul, it's the most vulnerable, courageous thing we'll ever do, but when we do this, our stories can be rewritten. I'm healed when I confess my struggles to you. Our hearts were made for freedom, but we have a prison around our hearts because we're petrified of each other. Living vulnerably doesn't mean that you're not going to be afraid. Being courageous doesn't mean that you won't feel fear. It's about rising up above it.

It's choosing to show up, despite how you feel. Imagine our children felt listened to? Understood by us? How could this rewire their brain? Where is anxiety in a home where a child is attuned to this way?

Your story doesn't have to be what it is. One out of every five people today struggles with a mental health issue. Knowing that we can transform one another's minds through attuning reminds me that there is hope to see this statistic significantly decrease.

Think of what this can mean for the problem of addiction. During the crisis in our home, I used to drink myself to sleep every night. When I got brave enough to tell a friend, my story was met with judgment and shame. They couldn't believe I would do such a thing. *You shouldn't be concerned about my drinking, but* why *I'm drinking,* I'd thought. I didn't think that taking up alcohol would be fun. I was drinking because I felt so much despair. I thought this crisis was now our reality for the rest of our lives.

It wasn't until a different friend said to me, "Connie, you've forgotten who you are. You're a warrior, an overcomer. I'm getting you up off the floor and I'm going to walk with you through this until you remember." Guess who hasn't drunk herself to sleep since? When my story was met with judgment, I drank even more than night. When my story was met with an empathetic listener who cared for me, my story changed. It seems so simple, but it's true that when we are loved, we become more lovable and capable of loving. One of my favourite children's books, *The Velveteen Rabbit*, says it best:

"Real isn't how you are made," said the Skin Horse. "It's a thing that happens to you. When a child loves you for a long, long time, not just to play with, but REALLY loves you, then you become Real."

"Does it hurt?" asked the Rabbit.

"Sometimes," said the Skin Horse, for he was always truthful. "When you are Real you don't mind being hurt."

"Does it happen all at once, like being wound up," he asked, "or bit by bit?"

"It doesn't happen all at once," said the Skin Horse. "You become. It takes a long time. That's why it doesn't happen often to people who break easily, or have sharp edges, or who have to be carefully kept. Generally, by the time you are Real, most of your hair has been loved off, and your eyes drop out and you get loose in the joints and very shabby. But these things don't matter at all, because once you are Real you can't be ugly, except to people who don't understand."[1]

Our family's future is ours to write. When we have the courage to walk into our story, we get to write the ending. This doesn't mean we have to be perfect. In fact, studies are showing more and more that even if we only get it right 30% of the time, our kids are going to be okay. This isn't an excuse not to do the hard work of making sense of our story so we can pass a better story down for our children, but it does take us off the hook to be perfect.

So, how do we help our children write a better story? The best way to help your children write a better story for themselves is to help your children make sense of their experiences. When a child is young, explaining to them a play-by-play of what happened in a situation helps their brain process an event. Perhaps they fell down off a playset. They are hurt and afraid. By explaining to them the details of what happened, they make sense of it.

"You were playing on the ground and then you decided to try to climb up the bars. You weren't quite big enough to reach the top, so you fell and hit your knee on the ground. Now we're making it all better with a hug and a band-aid."

Your child is less likely to let that experience traumatize them from the playground if you help them process what happened.

My mom helped me make sense of why I didn't have a father in my early childhood years. When I was just three years old, she explained to me that she fled domestic violence when I was only a year old. Of course, she explained this in a way that made sense to me at age three and in a way wouldn't traumatize me. I have never had issues with that part of my story because my mom helped me make sense of it when I was young. When my mom remarried when I was four years old, she helped me make sense of why my last name was changing, and about this new man in my life. This man she married became "my dad" in my heart because my mom took the time to walk me through the process.

Tell your children the story of situations and experiences to help them make sense of their world because stories help us make sense of our lives. When we share stories, it connects us and creates a sense of belonging and rootedness.

---

[1] Margery Williams, *The Velveteen Rabbit* (New York, NY: George H. Doran Company, 1922).

The best way to make sense of your story and help your children is to pay attention to emotions. Emotions are what frame our experiences. Emotions help us make meaning of situations we've faced. We'll remember what happened, but what we remember most is the emotion(s) attached to it. This is why two people can experience the same thing but remember it completely differently.

For example, let's say you and your partner enjoyed a date at that restaurant. Your partner loved it and couldn't stop raving about the time you had, while you remember what a disaster that evening was because your dress ripped and you spilled your drink, after which you felt embarrassed for the rest of the evening. Your partner wasn't embarrassed, so all they remember is the fun and laughter they experienced. But the emotion of embarrassment gave you a completely different memory and perception.

Being aware of the emotions we experience in different situations is key. Once you can name an emotion, you can also try to tame it. Noticing what situations cause anxiety or depression gives you power over it. Noticing where you are when you experience the most joy is equally important. When we're aware of our emotions and share them with our family, we deepen our connection with them.

When you've experienced something challenging, instead of moving on from the experience quickly because you want to forget it, stating to your family, "Wow, that was challenging wasn't it?" can help everyone in the family connect around the experience you just had together. Some in the family might agree, some might have had a different experience and now feel free to share, as well.

I'll never forget the time I was driving on a twelve-hour road trip with my oldest son. There was an accident on the highway that delayed us seven hours. This meant us having to find a hotel at midnight an hour away from our actual destination. Every hotel was booked, except for one for $250 for the night. At this point, we would be in the hotel for only six hours to sleep. We honestly couldn't afford it.

I began to cry, and when I cry, both my boys (and my husband) tend to freak out. They have no idea what to do with Mom when she's crying. It seems to cause them distress because they assume every time I cry, it's their fault. I helped my son process his discomfort by explaining, "I'm crying because I feel so overwhelmed. It's nothing you have done to cause this." He then felt more at ease. It helped him make sense of the situation as I named the emotion I was feeling. Naming emotion brings our mind from chaos to order.

We also help develop empathy in ourselves and our children when we are able to communicate emotions attached to experiences. When we identify with our children's emotions in a situation, they gain perspective. For example, when my oldest was in Grade Seven, he was getting sent to the principal's office daily for misbehaving. Everything in me wanted to rail into him about his behaviour. Instead, I began to take him through a process of what he was feeling.

"Son, are you feeling frustrated with school?"

"YES."

Then the floodgates opened as to why he was behaving the way he was, all due to how he was feeling. Naming the emotion helped my son make sense of why he was behaving the way he was. If I would have berated him about his behaviour, all he would have left with was the feeling that he is a "bad kid." After twenty years of working with at-risk youth, I'm convinced that all the "bad kids" out there really aren't bad at all. They haven't had anyone see past their behaviour to help them process what's really going on inside of them. Shame has no power over someone who has made sense of the emotions attached to experiences.

When we notice the emotions our children are facing, they feel understood. They know they belong and feel safe. This allows them to be able to rest. In order for someone to feel like they belong, they have to feel understood. When someone doesn't feel understood, you will see the worst side of them. People feel understood when we identify with their emotions. The reason we find this challenging at times is because of how we were treated in our homes regarding our emotions and behaviour.

In my home growing up, emotions were not welcome. Anger was altogether "bad" while displaying sadness in public was "an embarrassment." Even "overly excited" was to be toned down.

The way emotions were handled when we were young affects how we handle the emotions in our children. The more we learn to embrace emotions as being beautifully human and help our children process them, the more resilient our children will be. If we don't learn to do this, our children continue in the cycle of having their perception and reality distorted.

Any story you don't own for yourself will own you. Here are some questions to help you begin to dive into your story and create a new one for yourself and your children. Doing this is vital. You're going to want to ignore it. You're going to be tempted to skip ahead to the real "tools" in the book to help you manage your child's behaviour. Don't do it. If tools and books were going to help us manage our children's behaviour, it would have worked already. This is the key right here—making sense of your story so you can write a new one for your family. It's worth every ounce of effort. Be brave.

Here are some action steps to take:

- Notice your reactions. Don't judge them; simply notice them.
- Dig underneath your behaviour. Why do you respond that way?
- Think of an issue in your life that might be hindering your relationship.
- Write out your story.
- Who created you? What experiences and people have shaped who you are?
- Do you see anything that has been created that has distorted your perception?
- How do you see your perceptions influencing how you behave?
- Write a new story about what you want your life to be like.
- Think of three words that describe your relationship with your child. Are they similar to your relationship with your parents?

Here are some questions to ponder:

- What was your relationship with your parents like? What created connection in your home? What created disconnection?
- In what ways did you promise yourself you would never be like your parents? Are you the same way with your child?
- What did your parents do that made you angry? Afraid? Sad? Happy?
- Do you notice patterns in your upbringing that were like an echo chamber? Has it shaped your perception of the world? Is it different from how your partner, and/or your children, perceive things?
- Are you able to process and name emotions?
- Have you experienced grief, such as the loss of someone close to you, or a job? Perhaps moving cities? How has that affected you?
- Have you struggled with any addiction? What is underneath the addiction? What were you trying to numb or redeem?
- Have you experienced a toxic relationship or work environment? How has that affected you?

Chapter Eight
Peace in My Heart Translates to Peace in My Home

"You can't bathe anyone without peace in your hands."
(Jean Vanier, source unknown)

IT WAS A LONG, DARK YEAR. SENDING MY SON TO HIS ROOM WHILE HURLING INSULTS AND breaking things was so much easier than keeping him beside me. The first thing I needed to face in my heart was this: Peace would not translate to my home if it wasn't in my heart first. "Peaceful" is not how you would describe me. I move through life fast. I didn't realize that my ambition and drive were translating into my home as chaos. It also meant that any form of emotional dysregulation or outbursts from my son was a complete inconvenience to my day. I had things to do. I had no room in my schedule for his meltdowns. During the times of sitting with my son in the mess of his mental prison, I had no choice but to face myself. I had to get over the idea of looking for whom to blame. I was left to face myself in the mirror, wondering how I got here. As I reflected, I was reminded of what was happening in my life just before my son was born.

Before my son was born, we lived on the West Coast by the ocean, and I owned a dance studio. It was my dream. In that season of my life, I was living right in my sweet spot. I'll never forget the day my husband told me he was considering moving back to my home city to be with my mother. Just a few years earlier, my dad and grandma had both suddenly passed away, leaving my mom alone to take care of my grandpa, who had dementia. I knew it was the right thing to do, but I couldn't imagine letting go of a dream I had worked so hard to achieve. I was seven months pregnant when we moved into my mother's basement while my husband renovated my grandparents' home, where we would soon be living. These were some of the loneliest months I'd ever experienced. It was just me and my wiener dog while my husband worked fourteen-hour days. It gave me plenty of time to think about the heartache of leaving my dream behind. But I was determined to keep the dream alive. I had hired a manager to keep the studio running, which gave me purpose to continue to fuel the dream from afar.

I'll never forget the day I got the call when it all came crashing down. My son was only a few weeks old. It was a traumatic birth, he was colicky, we weren't sleeping, and I was having a hard time breastfeeding. My days were spent lonely on the couch watching the Home and Garden channel. That one day, my manager had called to say that the place we leased had changed the locks. She was standing outside the building with all the children ready to take the class (and parents who had paid for it). That was it; she quit right there. With no manager and no studio space, plus a mob of angry parents and disappointed children, my dream was officially over. There was nothing I could do. It was completely out of my control.

The first year of my son's life was one of the hardest years of disappointment I've ever faced. Everything piled up on me: my dream ending, sleepless nights with a colicky baby, arguments with my husband because we were both exhausted, and feeling isolated and alone. I didn't realize how much of a part this played in beginning our family's story. I had no peace in my heart. I drowned myself in the gym, finding a new purpose in becoming a fitness nut. I spent hundreds of dollars on clothes and items (that are in a garbage dump somewhere) just to fill the void I felt in my heart. I looked fulfilled on the outside, but peace was far from my heart. As you can guess, I had no foundation in my heart to handle the crisis we were about to experience with our son in the next few years.

Life with our son was hard. He went from a colicky baby to an unmanageable toddler, to an oppositional preschooler. As you've read earlier in the book, we finally got answers through a diagnosis when he was six years old. Fast-forward to our crisis when he was eight years old, a three-week stay in the hospital, and to coming home. I didn't realize how much this part of my story affected the way I parented him in those young years. I spent all of his infancy numbing the pain I felt. I had no peace. As I sat on the couch in tears while my son ripped me to shreds with his words during one of his outbursts, this truth was beginning to be formed inside of me: If I'm not peaceful, my *home* is not peaceful. Mental health starts with *me*, not with my children.

We don't realize that our unresolved issues cause distress in our minds, preventing us from being able to handle any emotional distress or unpredictable outbursts from our children—or anyone for that matter. This causes us to respond in ways that are often confusing and even sometimes frightening to our family. We think we're reacting to the present situation, but the truth is that we're reacting to something that's happened before. This is why we can appear to be "going off the deep end" with our response. In these moments, we have a choice: if we've made sense of our story, we can get a clear perspective on the present situation and respond appropriately.

If we haven't made sense of our story, it's "Mayday!! We're going down!" At this point, we're out of control. When we react this way often, we unintentionally make our children fearful and confused. This can show up as anxiety or even depression. It can increase oppositional and ADHD behaviours. The best thing we can do for our children is to make sense of our story for ourselves, and then help them make sense of our own story.

One time, driving on a road trip with my son, he was distraught and explained to me that, "No one else is going through what I go through." He was completely alone in his mental struggle and he felt I could never understand. Meanwhile, I'm thinking to myself, *Of course I understand! I'm your mother and I've worked with youth just like you for more than twenty years!*

But my attempt to explain to him how much I did (and do) understand made everything go downhill fast. It turned into a heated argument during which I was no longer responding to my son's need to be heard; I was responding to my need for my point to be understood.

"Why can't you just listen to me?!"

Mayday! Down I went, leaving both my son and me in tears.

When spiralling down in these situations, one of the best things we can do as parents is to stop interacting with our child. Until we gain perspective, it's only going to get worse. After taking a moment to make sense of what just happened, I reached for my son and said, "You're right. I don't understand" (all the while murmuring under my breath how much I do actually understand).

From his perspective, he needed me to simply acknowledge his feeling. I explained how frustrating that must have been for him for me not to hear him, and that I was sorry for the way I reacted. This seemed to bring peace to his mind. I concluded by saying, "Son, I might not understand, but I care. I care a lot about your feelings and what you're going through." Doing this allowed my son to avoid leaving the conversation feeling confused or unheard. It increased our connection.

When I first began to keep my son in the same room, telling him I would fight with him through his outbursts, he truly didn't believe me. He was leery of this new parenting "method." He was used to me reading parenting books and trying techniques on him to "fix" his behaviour. His little mind didn't know it, but it could pick up my counterfeit. We can have all the right tools in our toolkit. But if there is no peace in our hearts, it remains powerless. Our children are tired of our methods and techniques to "fix" them. They need us to show up and keep showing up and prove ourselves to build trust.

I had to take a hard look at my motive for wanting to help my son. Of course, it was because I wanted to see him whole and well, but it was also for *me*. I wanted to be able to walk down the mall without angry glares caused by my son's meltdowns. I wanted to be able to go through the supermarket without the fruit section becoming an obstacle course. I wanted the judgments from others to stop. I wanted my son to change for my benefit. I wanted to be able to go through my day without being interrupted by outbursts.

The truth is, anytime we try to fix someone for our benefit, not theirs, it's manipulation. Kids are amazing BS-o-metres. They know when something isn't authentic. They can't express it with words, but they certainly let us know by not cooperating with all our attempts to change them. When I would raise my voice, eventually leading to a fit of uncontrollable anger, it was because I was trying to fix him, and my attempts weren't working. I then would up the ante by lowering myself to name-calling—all to change his behaviour. At that point, any sense of reason was gone. The mature adult had left the building, leaving me looking like a two-year-old having a tantrum. There have been countless times during tantrums in our home (my husband and I experiencing them as well) when I've thought to myself, *Where are the adults?!*

I wanted my son to change for me. Once I realized this, I was able to work on managing my own anxiety, which was where my need to change him was coming from. In order to manage my anxiety, I needed to find peace again. I needed to make peace with the great disappointment I felt with life: the ending of my dream, the years of loneliness devoid of purpose, and a child given to me whom I felt I couldn't handle.

I thought it was my son's behaviour that was causing such distress, but it was actually the lack of peace I had. I would respond from a place of anger and frustration instead of a place of peace when my son was losing his mind because that's all you have when your heart is devoid of peace: anger and frustration. The greatest thing we can do as parents is to tend to the garden of our hearts. Our heart is where all life flows from. When our heart isn't doing well, neither are we or all those for whom we care. When we tend our hearts well, we protect the connection we have with our family and those closest to us. The greatest shame I have carried as a parent is the names I've called my son when my anger got the best of me.

Some of us believe that if we could just get our children to stop doing this, or quit behaving that way, that we wouldn't have such strong reactions, but that isn't true. Our reactions are a picture of how *we* are doing on the inside. Our reactions are our responsibility. They're not caused by others. It's hard to let go of the decisions our kids make and not make them our own. It's hard to separate our emotions from our children's emotions. There's nothing easy about separating yourself from the meltdown your toddler is having in the middle of the grocery store while all eyes are on *you*.

Once, my son refused to complete a project that was due the next day at school. I got all worked up, completely lost my cool, and tried everything to get him to complete the project. I uttered threats, I yelled, I took away every privilege. He outright refused and wasn't budging. After exhausting all my energy on trying to get him to complete this project, I realized that this was *his* decision, not *mine*. His decision didn't affect me at all. Didn't I pass Grade Six already?

Since then, I've learned the art of letting my son own his decisions. This has brought peace back to my soul. I don't heartlessly leave him out to dry when he makes poor decisions. The opposite is true. I'm able to gracefully walk alongside him (most days—let's admit, no one is perfect), assisting him through living the pain or joy of his decisions. This is key to having a child with opposition. They thrive when they have control over their decisions. (More on this later in the book.)

Measuring how well we're doing as parents by our children's behaviour is unrealistic, depressing, and a sure way to rob us of our peace. I've discovered I'm not as flexible as I'd like to think I am. When things don't go the way I plan I become tense, frustrated, and anxious. I'm used to going at a fast pace; therefore, I get annoyed when I'm interrupted. One of the greatest ways I've seen more peace come to my heart is by slowing down my life. (More on this later in the book, as well.)

One of the other keys to peace I have found through my journey is that calm is not the road to peace. I can search for calm, only to find myself becoming all wound up. I'm not opposed to methods that help us calm down, such as mindfulness exercises. What I find frustrating is when I expect those exercises to bring peace to my soul. I can have an amazing hour of peaceful meditation and prayer, only to wake up to the reality of my children's screams and fighting. Where does the calm go? Right out the flippin' window!

I can take deep breaths before responding to a situation, only to find my children have sent my mind off the deep end before reaching the third breath. Now I'm also upset because they've disrupted and stolen the calm state I was just experiencing a moment ago. How will I get it back when I have no time to light candles and take deep breaths for an hour?! Calm disappoints me. I gain it for a moment only to lose it. My mood is dictated by whether I feel I have calm or whether it has been taken from me. At that moment, my children seem as though they are the enemy. They are the culprits of why I don't have calm in my life. They steal it from me.

Really? Nope—bogus. No one steals anything from me. You can't steal something if it's not there in the first place. Calm isn't something I *have*; it's something I experience from time to time.

A peaceful heart is not developed through practices to achieve "calm." I've discovered that joy creates a level of peace that can't be stolen in moments of chaos. Not happiness, but joy. Joy is different from happiness because it doesn't rely on things, experiences, or people to create it. Joy is an emotion, much like shame, that runs deeper than other emotions. It's embedded in us through choosing to find pleasure in the moments of our day.

It's finding delight again in my children's faces instead of looking at all the things that frustrate me about them. It's seeing the beauty in the simple and allowing gratitude to fill my heart. Joy doesn't mean I'm laughing or smiling all the time; it means I'm able to find contentment in every situation. I've noticed through years of heartache and crisis that the times I have had the most peace was when I would choose joy. The pursuit of calm left me frustrated and grasping to feel more of it, only to be left empty. Joy never disappoints. It remains, even when the day gets out of control.

What do you do when there *is* no joy? When life has brought you to a dark place? When just getting out of bed is hard? Remember, joy isn't happiness. It's deeper than a feeling. It's choosing to see the moments in your day worthy of gratitude. I have personally experienced days, months, and seasons during which there's more dark than light, more pain than hope. Where does joy fit in during those times? In the small things, and taking it day by day, or even moment by moment. Slowly, over time, the light grows. Today's culture doesn't value the time it takes for seasons of our lives to change. We market a cheap message that tells us happiness is our daily right. Instagram doesn't tell us how long it takes for joy to become a part of us by the daily discipline of looking for that "one thing" to be thankful for that is often in the mundane. Make it a daily practice to find beauty in the simple, and you'll see joy become easy to find. Joy is developed through persevering through heartache. I can't explain it. It just happens. The times I've attempted to think up joy "on the spot" have been futile, but I can look back on every hardship I've faced in my life to find joy as a reward at the end. These heartaches develop a level of perseverance, character, and hope that I can't create on my own.

In case you missed the keys to peace in this chapter, let me summarize:
- Separate yourself from your children's decisions.
- You can't bring someone closer if you don't bring yourself closer first. Make sense of your story so you can write a new one.
- You manage your emotions first.
- Tend to the garden of your heart first.
- Rediscover joy.

Chapter Nine

You Don't Control Your Kids

ONE DAY, I WAS AT THE PARK WITH MY BOYS WHEN THEY WERE YOUNG. ANOTHER MOM came storming up to me with anger in her eyes, telling me that my boys had done something to offend her. I honestly can't remember what it was.

I do remember is her saying, "Why don't you control your children?"

I turned to her and said, "I don't *control* anyone."

That didn't go over well.

This statement doesn't go over well with any parent at first. Certainly, we want to teach our children to be respectful, but *how* we do that is not through control. When I seek to control another person and they don't comply, I resort to tactics that are less than worthy.

Have you ever had a day with your child when you've pulled out every tool, every strategy, etc., and they *still* aren't listening? You think to yourself the only thing left to do is to hit the kid. This is probably why there are harsh words and physical violence in homes; it's our attempt to control.

No parent wakes up wanting to yell at—or hit—their child. It just happens when we can't seem to get a grip on our child. We are told by our culture to "control" our children, but that's the last thing we need to hear.

The only person we *control* is ourselves. When we focus on our own behaviours and regulation, we can respond rather than react.

I recall another time at a park with my boys. My youngest pulled my oldest's hair and out came some colourful language. There were toddlers everywhere.

Every mother in the park gasped in unison at my son's language, and gasps turned from angry glares at my son to me. I was utterly embarrassed. I wanted to disappear. Everything in me wanted to go up and scold my son in front of all of those judging mothers, giving them the retribution they desired.

But that day, I didn't. I looked at my son, who was welling up with tears as he realized what he had done. My boy who felt humiliated for making a mistake and knew he had a mob of angry moms ready to pounce, including his own mother.

I went up to him, and told him, "It's okay. We all make mistakes."

And then I walked past the angry mob with my boys in hand. This is the one day I got it right out of dozens of times. Those other times, I reacted harshly towards my children out of my desire to please other people and to *control* my children.

I'm not saying my son's language was okay. I'm also not saying we should let our children off scot-free for their poor choices. Rather, what I'm saying is that when they make a mistake or any choice that isn't great, the first person we must control is ourselves. We control *our* reactions.

I wanted to lose it on my son that day in the park, but instead, I controlled my response I was able to talk through the situation with my son calmly, reinforcing what isn't appropriate for language and behaviour. He learned a lesson without shame getting the upper hand in his heart.

When we focus on controlling our reactions first, we're more at peace with our children's mistakes. We realize that they're learning.

Think back to your own childhood and teen years. How many times did you make crazy mistakes? Did someone attempt to control you or, through those mistakes, did they open up conversations and opportunities to learn and grow?

Connection, not *control*, must be our goal.

The ones who need connection the most are often the ones with the most challenging behaviours. Resilient children are ones with positive connections, those who have a safe place to land at home, school, and in the community.

Rather, this is a problem for children who display defiance. They're the ones who need connection the most, but they're the least likely to get it. They have prickles and a face that says, "Screw off!" That scares people away.

Oh, what a gift to find those who can see the gold past the prickles. Those precious people can see a prickly child transform into a beautiful, beloved child.

In all my years of teaching, I've always been drawn to these kinds of students. Now, being the mother of a child such as this, my heart prays daily for someone to see the beauty in my son and pull it out so he has hope to become beloved as well.

I guarantee that no child wakes up in the morning wanting to be a jerk. My son said something powerful to me the other day: "When I'm angry, people look different."

Oppositional children are special. They remind us not to blindly conform to everything people tell us. Their determination to gain autonomy and choice is an incredible opportunity for us to see how distorted some of the ways we work with children can be. They call out our crazy need for control and shake us up.

I personally don't believe in the label "Oppositional Defiance Disorder." First, what a horrible label to be given. It says to a child, "You are oppositional. You are defiant. You have a disorder." What good does this do for the child? Even us? We then only see them through that lens and treat them as such. It's a lose-lose-lose situation for the parent, the teacher, and the child.

Second, if a child truly is oppositional, you would see opposition from them all the time. The truth is, opposition only appears in certain situations, mostly when the child feels like they're being *controlled*. My oldest son will show all kinds of opposition when he feels like he's being imposed upon.

Of course, this is a real problem when I'm trying to get him out the door and he has decided he doesn't want to go anywhere, but other times, he makes me stop to think about why I want him to do certain things. He makes me question what I consider "normal." He brings up some good points to what we put up with as a society.

What a gift.

One time, I picked my son up after school when he was in Grade Seven. He stormed into the car and shouted, "Screw feminism!"

Hold the phone. I asked him if he believed in equal rights for women, and this was his response: "Of course, Mom. Just don't strip me of mine to get them."

I was wowed by my son's perspective. His opposition to having ideologies imposed on him that take away his rights that day was a gift of opening my eyes regarding this social issue. I left that conversation with a new perspective. We don't gain our rights by stripping others of theirs. It's in moments like that when I'm proud my son isn't a conformist.

The greatest advice I have for parents with "oppositional" children is to learn the art of differentiation—not letting your child's emotions affect yours.

One day, during an episode of great frustration with my son's refusal to cooperate, I asked myself, "Why does opposition bother me so much?" I realized it was because I wanted easy cooperation from my children. I didn't want them to question me or why things are the way they are. I realized how much I actually like—and even—need control. When we're in control of our own emotions, we can properly handle others' hard emotions.

For parents struggling with strong-willed children, do not give in to the desire to put them in a timeout—it will only backfire. These kids will end up feeling alone, isolated, and disconnected. Instead, keep them with you. Bring them closer.

I have seen my son take on this "me against the world" attitude many times. It always precedes being misunderstood by me, a teacher, or any adult.

In my son's seventh-grade year, he had a teacher whom he believed did not like him. I'm not sure if she liked him or not; however, I do know he was being sent to the principal's office *every single day*. When I would drop him off at school in the morning, he would say to me, "I'll probably be in the principal's office by noon." He was right. My son's approach to a teacher not liking him is very different from my approach.

If I thought a teacher didn't like me, then I was determined to *make* that teacher like me. I went into overachiever mode with my people-pleasing skills. Not my son. When he thinks a teacher doesn't like him, he's determined to prove to them every reason that they shouldn't. He becomes more disruptive in class and will do anything to prove their theory that he is, in fact, a "bad kid." I tried talking to him about it. I had numerous meetings with the principal and his teacher. Nothing was working; no one was winning. So, in spring this past year, I pulled him out of school for homeschooling.

When I tried to talk to my son about his behaviour in school, I was only met with his determination to respond however he felt he needed to. So I told him that whatever he decided to do, he needed to own his decision. This has been the most powerful tool I have in working with my son, especially as he has become older. I explained to him if he couldn't make better decisions that avoided him getting into trouble, then we would be bringing him home. He would lose the "privilege" of school.

Never in a million years did I ever think I would threaten to take away the "privilege" of school. My son loved going to school to be with his friends, and wanted to continue going to school to be with them. He chose to continue to be disruptive, but he also started to see his own negative pattern. In the end, it was he who asked to be homeschooled, simply because he didn't know how to make better choices for himself.

That's what we want with an oppositional child—to bring them to the place where they can see the effects of their choices and for them to make better ones. I was proud of my son's self-awareness.

My son thrives with homeschooling because he has more control over his education. He decides *when* he does school, *when* he finishes, and *what* he studies. I have a list of requirements he needs to fulfill, and then he figures out how he's going to do that. Many would think this is a recipe for disaster, but he is the most organized and motivated I've ever seen when he's given control over his day.

I'll never forget when my son said to me when he was in Grade Three, "I don't need to go to school. I can learn everything I need to know on YouTube." The funny thing is, he's right.

When my son was in elementary school, I would often tell him, "You can either listen to adults now or when you're older." There were many days I would explain to him that in life, you can learn to manage under rules of when it's bedtime or what activity comes next when you're young, or you can do it when you're older. Mental health hospitals, rehabilitation centres, and even prison, where those who can't cooperate end up, will have their lives dictated to them. Other people tell you when you can come and leave, when you can eat, what you will eat, where you will sleep, and what you can have in possession with you. With freedom comes maturity needed to handle that kind of responsibility.

As young as my son was, this seemed to resonate with him. He didn't want to grow up being more controlled. I could see the wheels in his mind turning. As my son grew older, working with his opposition has been easier. We've had great conversations about how the word "No" shuts down connection, ideas, fun, and hearing one another.

My son's opposition shows up in times when he feels out of control, which actually feels scary for him. It also rises when he doesn't feel understood or heard, and when he needs someone to come beside him and sit with him in his emotional dysregulation, no matter how uncomfortable that might feel for the parent or teacher.

Our kids can't do this without our help. Too many times, adults want children to deal with their emotions on their own. We need to flip this. We need to allow them to own the decisions they make, and help them regulate their emotions along the way.

Connection is the only way to get through to an oppositional child. If you don't connect with your ODD student or child, they'll begin to act out (only confirming what you thought of them) when connection is all they were wanting. Ironically, it would have rerouted them. Connection is our only hope of getting through to them.

My son still has the occasional meltdown. What does an episode look like? Yelling, cursing, throwing, and smashing things, and refusing to listen to any instruction. This used to be our life on a daily basis, and I would feel such despair over how to deal with it. I'm thankful that this is now a rare occasion because dealing with it is exhausting.

We've come a long way. While I used to deal with my son's outbursts by sending my son to his room in between my own yelling dysregulation, now I bring my son closer. It looks like this:

- not allowing his emotion to affect my own
- keeping a firm but kind tone and consistency, no matter how hard he tries to push me away
- allowing my son to own his decisions (During one episode, my son completely messed up our basement. I didn't even look at it. I simply told him he needed to clean it up before anything else could happen. Believe me, cleaning up the mess he made was quite a task. Making him own his decisions has been the best thing for him to rethink them next time.)
- reminding my son I love him, but that this swearing or name-calling is not how we communicate to one another
- brief sentences until he is calm, then talking about what happened (you can't reason with someone when they're dysregulated)
- reminding myself that these types of reactions will not break our connection; however, they won't be tolerated
- hugs and time together when it's all over and forgiveness is granted

I believe in doing this time and again for the long haul is what has caused such a dramatic change in my son from daily episodes like this to only a few times a year. You don't send the hurting away; you bring them closer.

Oppositional defiance can be described as resistance to the feeling of being forced. It can often look like laziness, negativity, or hostility. You will always see opposition rise when connection isn't the goal. When all you want is to get your children to behave, you're sure to experience resistance from oppositional children. The more connected your child feels to you, the more they trust you, the more they will be willing to cooperate because of the trust and connection that has been built.

Many times we label these children as "rebellious" or "strong-willed" or "stubborn." Oppositional children have a hard time complying when they don't feel the adult likes them, when they feel misunderstood, when they feel ideas are being imposed on them. They seem to want more autonomy earlier in life than most children. Parents of these children need to create space for choice that is age-appropriate. It's a problem when we see our children as "rebellious" or wanting control, because then we try harder to overpower them, which, of course, works exactly opposite from what we desire.

We often forget to see our oppositional child as a child who still needs our help. Instead, we lock ourselves into power struggles that create more disconnection instead of connection. How many battles have I engaged in with my son that have ended with us both slamming doors or in tears only because I forgot what his opposition was showing he needed—*autonomy* and *choice*? Some days, it's not my son's opposition I need to worry about; rather, it's *mine*.

> Even though you try to put people under some control, it is impossible. You cannot do it. The best way to control people is to encourage them to be mischievous. Then they will be in control in its wider sense. To give your sheep a spacious meadow is the way to control him. So it is with people; first let them do what they want and watch them. This is the best policy. To ignore them is not good, that is the worst policy. The second worst is trying to control them. The best one to watch them, just watch them, without trying to control them. (Shunryu Suzuki Roshi, source unknown)

Here are some practical tips on how to work with an oppositional child. I have practiced each and every one of these, and they work brilliantly.

Keep *connection* the goal first and foremost before seeking to change or control their behaviour.

- Remember, compliance isn't your goal. There are many children who nod yes on the outside but are defiant on the inside.
- Remember to not take your child's opposition personally. It's not about you, or your parenting skills; it's about them resisting being imposed upon.
- Don't be shocked when your child is defiant, but work to respond firmly but kindly. Whenever I've reacted and yelled, it's only made things worse.

- Pick your battles. There are so, so many battles. You can't engage in them all. Pick the ones that really matter and let other matters slide for the time being. I have found I have had to wait about six months to get something that matters achieved for my son before moving on to something else we need to work through. Every six to twelve months, we "level up." For example, when he turned twelve, my battle was getting him to shower every day. After that became a habit, we moved on to something else.
- Teach your child to respectfully advocate for themselves. My son feels heard when I don't shut him down. Not all opposition is wrong; sometimes our kids bring up some valid points. What needs to be worked on the delivery—to not yell or insult to express themselves. Try this: "I will listen to what you have to say if you can say it calmly without insults."
- Recognize your own opposition. Many times, my son's opposition flares up when I'm refusing to be flexible or listen.
- Remember, resilience is in the repair. It's important to repair every time you have an argument or rupture in connection with your child. (More on this later in the book.)

Teach your child to own their decisions. If it's autonomy they want, give it to them and allow them to own the outcomes. Debrief how it goes. Oppositional children learn best through their own mistakes. Of course, do this in line with what's appropriate for their age and development. The more you give them the opportunity for this in some aspects of their life, the more willing they may be to comply in situations in which they don't have a choice.

Then there's ADHD. Children with ADHD also come with challenging behaviours we like to control. My son said to me one day, "If ADHD is such a gift, why do you suppress it with making me take pills? Is there something wrong with my personality?"

In all my years of working in resilience, I've heard many kids say the same thing. They often feel targeted by teachers, misunderstood by adults, bullied by other kids, and then wonder if there's something wrong with them. Kids with ADHD don't have the same level of skills as others to be able to reason, so we can't expect this. When children are understood, they become their most courageous self that can reach their potential. Look for the gifts in your ADHD child, and they will begin to believe the best about themselves.

There is much confusion regarding what ADHD actually is. When we see a child who has a lot of energy and can't sit still, we label them as having ADHD.

However, most children have a lot of energy and can't sit still. I honestly don't believe sitting in desks all day works well for many children. I remember talking to a group of fifth-graders about the power of movement and stated, "Could you imagine if we just sat all day? We would shrivel up."

A fifth-grade boy yelled out, "That's what school is like!"

ADHD is a lack of attention, the inability to control impulses, tuning out, or hyperactivity (Attention Deficit Hyperactivity Disorder). Those with ADHD may fidget, talk a lot, lack social skills, not be able to finish their thoughts, be unable to make small talk, or are overachievers. I have ADHD. My husband used to call me "chaotic." That's exactly how it feels to be around someone who has ADHD.

I become insecure about some of the effects of ADHD in my life. I have to work extra hard at organizing my thoughts and remembering things.

I remember being in the lineup at the passport office. The number they would call when it was my turn was sixty-three. For some reason, numbers don't compute well in my brain, so I repeated my number three times to myself before I dove into the book I was reading. Somewhere in the moment between repeating the number sixty-three for the last time and picking up my book, my mind decided to remember the number sixty-four instead. I don't know how that happens, but this is something I experience often. I heard the number sixty-three called three times. *Who's the idiot who forgot their number?* I wondered. Then I looked down at my paper and noticed it was me.

This is what ADHD looks like in my world.

It's nearly impossible for someone with ADHD to pay attention when they have little interest in the subject. Yet, when they're very interested in something, they could focus on it for hours. This confuses parents because then they assume they could apply this same skill to all matters. This isn't the case. We love to throw medication at kids with ADHD, completely overlooking how much today's culture contributes to the problem. Fast pace, information overload, social media, email, texts, etc.

There are days when I find myself becoming shaky after checking my emails, messages on Facebook and Instagram, as well as phone calls and incoming texts. I find it hard to concentrate when my days are filled with meetings and long to-do lists. It very quickly feels like I'm spiralling out of control. All of this feels stressful and affects my mental state. I wonder what the state of my brain would be if it all was taken away, and I was left with a life without social media, emails, texts and overwhelming to-do lists?

I'll tell you what it looks like. It doesn't look like ADHD.

I personally have made some major life shifts in my life and home. I have cut my social media time to only certain moments in my day. I respond to emails once a day. I've cut my to-do list down to three manageable tasks a day. I work less than I ever have, but I'm more focused than ever. I don't run here and there to extracurricular activities with my kids. I keep our lives as slow and simple as possible. I homeschool my son and don't notice an ounce of his ADHD. There are busier seasons, but I make sure they don't last long—a few weeks at most. My children and I show very little signs of ADHD in this simple life we've created. Interesting.

Adjusting the environment for someone with ADHD makes all the difference. When I homeschool my son, we're rarely sitting. He learns the way he chooses; he picks what he wants to learn. I have no behavioural issues at home with him, but at school, he was getting sent to the principal's office daily for being "too distracting."

For me personally, I would daydream in school and miss important instructions. I couldn't focus. In my entrepreneurial work I've chosen for myself, I have no problems focusing on and executing tasks. Those of us with ADHD were never meant to fit inside a box. The problems we encounter occur when we try to box-in those with ADHD. Unfortunately, this only makes those who have it feel like there is something wrong with them. We can't allow this. Those with ADHD are often the movers, shakers, and outside thinkers our society needs.

Those of us with ADHD also have many weaknesses. For example, I always underestimate how long something will actually take. I've had to learn to over-budget time so I don't frustrate people around me waiting for a task to be completed. I have also had to work very hard at my own self-regulation. I am triggered easily with emotion. My inability to remain calm has caused me to react to my children. I also struggle with impulse control. For me, that has shown up mostly as spending too much money. I've never tried drugs because I know that my highly addictive personality could get hooked easily. I also am quite vague on details. All of these weaknesses I have just described are classic ADHD struggles. It's not because we "won't," it's because we "can't." However, ADHD is an issue of brain development—not an illness. ADHD is something I *have*, not something I *am*. This means it's manageable, and those like me can learn regulation, impulse control, and organization. What it takes is an environment that allows for it, and some self-discipline to learn.

I've been asked numerous times what causes ADHD. I don't think you'll like the answer. Above the way our culture functions as a whole, we have to go back and look at what ADHD stands for: Attention Deficit, a deficit of attention. Many experts agree that the lack of attention a child receives as an infant from their primary caregiver delays the development of the brain circuitry that's required to regulate, control impulses, and organize.

Learning this was a hard pill for me to swallow because when my son was born, I was not as attuned to him as I wanted to be. I had just moved to a new city, I was lonely and isolated, my husband was off working twelve to fourteen hours a day, and the dream of my dance studio came crashing down.

The actual, physical birth of my son was rough; then, he was then a colicky baby who wouldn't breastfeed. We weren't sleeping and I felt resentment that my life revolved around him. I loved my baby boy—I really did. I would have done anything for him, but I realize that throughout much of his infancy, I would look right past him. There wasn't a lot of eye-to-eye contact, and when there was, he would have only seen a cloud of disappointment, not regarding him, but in the season I was experiencing in my life.

Don't get me wrong—I met his every need. I woke up when he was hungry, which was many times in the night. I changed him, I fed him, I smiled at him. But even being with a mother who was physically present for him, as an infant, he could sense my emotional turmoil. He knew I was devoid of delight. There's no way I could ever fix this even if I wanted to. This is the reality for many mothers struggling with depression or a season of grief or disappointment.

What's unfortunate is that the more stressed and depressed I became that year, the more I would try to mask it. I couldn't deny I was becoming more irritable with my son's opposition as he grew, more frustrated with his inability to listen, and angrier with his behaviour. I would read book after book on parenting, when my own heart was what I needed to be tending to. The emotional turmoil in me was the undercurrent of all my reactions. Nothing would change unless I had a hard look at me first.

Learning about the importance of those early years and early bonding brought despair to my heart. *So I have caused my son's ADHD?* How could one season of my life have such an impact on my son's entire life and future? I can't begin to tell you the anger I felt, the sadness, the despair. But the truth is, I didn't want to face myself.

In a moment of grief, I heard a voice in my heart saying, "But God... But hope!" That voice gave me the courage to not throw this theory out the window, but to look at all of this with a fresh set of eyes. If neuroscience states that attachment during infancy can wire the brain, then attachment can also rewire the brain at any stage of life! The truth is, the brain is always mouldable. There's more hope than we know. The connection we give to our children at any stage matters more than we think. I let all new mothers know what I wish I would have, that attuning to their baby isn't meaningless.

Every time we connect with our child—no matter how old they are—it is doing something significant.

What many parents don't realize is that no matter how much love we feel for our child, it doesn't mean that the love is translating to our child. Our children don't know our loving motives unless that love is felt by them. When our children don't feel loved, they might misbehave or go over and above to gain our approval. This starts a very young cycle of feeling misunderstood, which leads to all kinds of instability in the mind. Issues like anxiety, depression, opposition, and ADHD can flare up when someone doesn't feel understood. It creates shaky ground on which to stand.

The emotional environment in which a child is raised affects ADHD. While we parents are reading books and listening to podcasts about the top three ways to manage our children, what they really need is a safe, supportive home in which parents have learned the art of self-regulation. The tension we feel inside gets passed to our children. Infants don't translate words; they translate emotions being communicated. Children feel our stress. In order to manage them, we need to manage ourselves first. Children also can sense our attitude towards them. If we feel annoyed or frustrated towards them, they know.

Children with ADHD are sensitive. This doesn't mean we can't feel these emotions. We're parents, after all (our children will annoy us), but if our overall attitude is one of resentment and seeing the child as a nuisance, that has an impact on their brain. The emotional environment we provide for our children teaches them how to see the world around them.

At times, my son would say to me, "Stop yelling!" The fact is, in these moments, I wasn't yelling. My voice was firm, but not raised. I found this interesting, as he knew what yelling sounded like. I would often yell, so it surprised me that when I was finally learning to be firm, but kind, that my son would still say I was yelling. ADHD children pick up tension and frustration. It can seem as loud to them as yelling. When I was firm, I was also frustrated. My son knew this, interpreting it as yelling.

This is tricky to navigate, because frustration isn't wrong to feel, and speaking firmly is needed. What's important to build is a level of connection so that when correction is needed, there's been enough trust built for the child to know that just because we are frustrated doesn't mean we don't love them. As my son often says to me, "Mom, when I feel you're disappointed in me, it literally destroys me inside." It's important not to criticize their oversensitivity or accuse them of "just wanting attention." Sensitive children can become hard to deal with when they don't feel the sensitivity inside them is understood by their parents. This can often show up as opposition.

My marriage has affected the emotional state of my son the most. When my marriage was on the brink of ending, my son's emotional sensitivity was at an all-time high. His ADHD was through the roof, his opposition in full throttle. He would often experience stomach pains. I didn't realize it at the time, but my son was reflecting in his body and behaviour the emotional atmosphere we were creating for him. After counselling, medication, and a ton of techniques, nothing has helped our son's emotional state more than our marriage improving. I do believe that the counselling and medication were needed, but we can't overlook the importance of working on our relationship with our partner and doing whatever it takes to create an emotionally safe environment for our children in which to thrive.

In today's world, we have forgotten the foundations of being rooted in the relationships we call home. We need to come back to this foundation, scrap all our strategies and techniques to get this right first, then focus on the proper tools. We're on the right track, we just have it backwards. And we wonder why our kids are still suffering.

"Can parents actually create the kind of ideal environment in which their children can thrive? Is this even possible?!" you might be wondering.

It's both unrealistic and depressing to assume we have to be perfect in order for our kids to be mentally healthy. I think it misses the point entirely. Our children need secure, safe environments that aren't overly stressful. That tells me that instead of striving for perfection, I need to be using that same energy to create calm in my home. This means becoming vigilant on all that is robbing myself and my family of things that steal our peace. This calls for a full-out rebellion on busyness, toxic work environments, toxic school atmospheres, etc., and creating a structure where peace can be cultivated in our homes.

It means getting real with myself and my stress level every day. I need to have my own quiet time each day to evaluate how my heart is doing and make the necessary changes. The changes we have made in our home have not been easy. It's taken more bravery than I've ever known to lay my pride down to work on my marriage. It's taken courage for me not to care what others think and take my son out of school to homeschool. I've disappointed more people than I can count by saying "no" to outings and activities that take me away from my home. But all of these decisions have helped my family more than I expected.

Here are some practical tips on how to work with your ADHD child:

1. Scrap the timeouts. Timeouts only serve to increase your child's anxiety because they are separated from you. We can't expect them to regulate on their own. Your child with ADHD might also have a hard time remembering why they are in a timeout, causing confusion. Instead, bring them closer, keeping them in the same room as you. Let them calm down and then walk them through what happened, like telling a story, and invite them to come up with solutions with you.

2. Create space in your life for your children's reactions. There is nothing more inconvenient than a meltdown or a child not listening when you're in a rush. Start their morning routine earlier to allow for time for this to potentially happen. Wake up earlier than your children for your own quiet time. Prepare yourself mentally and emotionally for anything that will go haywire that day. Kids need to know we can hold their big emotions. This is key for them learning to self-regulate. Learn to expect that things will not go according to your plan. Be flexible. This way, you're being *proactive* rather than *reactive*.

3. You are the one responsible for your relationship with your child. It's not their responsibility to create a safe emotional atmosphere for themselves. They're not to blame for a home that feels chaotic. That's on us, the adults. It's hard if we've never been properly parented to know how to be the adult in a relationship, but for the sake of our children, we must learn that nothing happens in our homes without our permission. We are the gatekeepers. If things have gone out of control, we are the only ones who are able to bring it all back into alignment. Children who have been given the burden of this responsibility are unable to grow past dysfunction. Children experience humiliation when we make them take initiative and responsibility for our relationship. We must show them a better way.

4. Create connection when all is calm. When your child isn't needing correction, or demanding attention, use that time to build trust and create connection by interacting with your child. Laugh. Do something silly,

fun, or even just relaxing. It will fill their cup so when it comes time to correct them, their cup is full enough for you to do so. Too often, we correct when their cup is empty, only causing them to sink further into emotional dysregulation, which causes them not to be unable to hear or receive the correction that we're giving.

5. Don't judge your child for their limitations. There's nothing more shameful than to be judged or blamed for things you can't control. The judgments of our parents when we're young are often carried with us into our adult life. If someone would have told me to "just get over" my depression when my son was born, not only would I not have been able to do so, I would have sunk further into depression because now, I was reminded of what a failure I was as a mother. The same goes for our children with ADHD. If we criticize our children by saying, "What's wrong with you?" they sink further away from the regulation we want them to have. Instead, tell them you are willing to walk with them and help them solve things that are hard for them.

6. Avoid interactions with your child when you are angry. As much as you can, remove yourself to become calm. Explain to your child that you need to calm down so that they understand. The problem that occurs when we don't manage our anger is that our children often feel they are walking on eggshells around us and learn techniques to avoid us, rather than connect with us.

7. Make the brave changes needed in your home and life to create the atmosphere your child needs to thrive. Be willing to do whatever it takes. Rebel against what our culture deems as "normal." This "normal" culture is destroying our children. I'm not saying take them out of school, I'm saying be willing to evaluate every aspect of your life and see where peace is being stolen from you and make those necessary changes. It will be unique for each and every family. If ADHD children are ultra-sensitive to negative emotional environments, it also means they are equally responsive to the positive environments that the adults can build for them.

8. Control yourself. We can often find ourselves behaving no differently from our children when we don't manage our own emotions. Self-regulation is the ability to manage our own anxiety. We manage ourselves before we manage anyone else. It's not our children's fault if we become dysregulated. Their behaviour does not determine yours; you determine

yours. It's our default as parents to want to control behaviour when we experience anxiety. Be intentional to seek to look inside and control yourself first.

9. What we need to do for our children is to stop trying to control their behaviour and control our own. We don't "fix" our children's behaviour; we fix the environment we are creating for them. We need to change our hearts, not our techniques. Parenting is not a skill; it's a relationship. We need to do whatever it takes to cultivate and protect that relationship. We need our children to know deep in their hearts that we choose *them*, day after day, because they belong and are loved. When connection is strong with us and our children, their minds become organized.

What about anxiety? Dealing with anxiety is tough. It seems to be everywhere today. Youth are struggling with social pressures that many of us didn't have to face with social media. There's much more pressure to do well in school because university entrance is now more competitive than ever. Parents are stressed, and children as young as five are struggling with anxious thoughts.

I believe in clinical anxiety. I know it's real, but I also know it can be put in its place. Anxiety looks like the primary issue, but when you look underneath, the issue is far deeper. Anxiety is an alarm stating that something is wrong inside of us or within our environment. Much of today's anxiety could be based on shame. Shame is developed through our experiences, environments, and belief systems. Shame sounds like this: "I don't have what it takes for this." "I don't think I can face my schoolmates tomorrow." "I can't do anything right at work." "I can't pass that test." Shame isn't the only matter possibly under anxiety. There's more. Anxiety is never alone; it's always accompanied by something we don't see. No one wakes up anxious for no reason.

The rise in anxiety in youth and parents has also come hand in hand with a decline of connection in families. Home is a place of roots and wings. When a child doesn't have the safety of a family to root them when hard times hit, they can't develop wings. They become prey to shame, feeling displaced, and numb where addictions wait to fill their void. In order for a young person to become resilient, they need the home to be their safe space where they receive the nurturing they need to face the world. Most youth today don't have that.

Giving our kids everything they want is also making them anxious. One of the problems with children getting what they want all the time is that they don't learn distress tolerance, which is key to resilience and overcoming anxiety. We need to remember that just because it's Christmas, doesn't mean our children are entitled to everything on their list.

We live in the land of choice as well. Kids can watch whatever they want, whenever they want. The Internet is always available. Netflix gives hundreds of choices that can be viewed at one click. Children's minds don't know how to process so much choice, as well as the ability to get whatever they want when they want it. It both confuses and overwhelms the mind.

School is causing an incredible source of anxiety for young people. Before I continue, I want to be upfront about how I feel about teachers. I'm so proud of them. They are heroes in my books. They're often asked to go beyond the call of duty to work extra hours, which takes them away from important things like prep or rest. They have large class sizes, with over half of the students with special needs requiring individual programs. The average professional lifespan of a new teacher is only five years. Many enter the profession wanting to make a difference only to find themselves covered in red tape that prevents them from doing so. They leave the profession for their own mental health.

Traditional school doesn't work for my son. One year, he claimed to be sick for over half the school year. When he did go, my husband would sometimes have to carry him over his shoulder to the car. Anxious kids have to overcome many obstacles at school. It's hard for them to learn anything when they are living in the back of their brain—the space in our brain where we are in a state of fight or flight. You can't reason in this state, let alone learn anything. This only increases their anxiety because often that means they are behind. They find homework overwhelming. They worry about their marks. Add social pressures on top of it all and it can seem too much. Social pressures are beginning to form in the early state of Grade Two!

We can't expect students with their mind full of negative thoughts to function. We need to ease their anxiety. This is tricky for teachers because of all the barriers they face, but we must come alongside them to help them figure out how.

I counted the days my son came home from school upset. There were more days than not. He explained to me he was feeling more depressed as each day passed. One day we arrived at the doors of the school and he just couldn't go in. I didn't make him go; instead, when we got home, I asked him to write out all the things he could handle at school in one column and all the things he felt that he couldn't handle in another column. He had only three things he could handle written (one of which was "leaving") and two pages of what he honestly felt he couldn't handle. Much of what he wrote in the "can't handle" column, he also couldn't control.

I like to redirect my kids to think about what they *can* control in various situations, rather than focusing on what's disempowering them. We adults often forget that as a child, a lot of things are out of your control. As an adult, I can make a choice of where I live and work, with whom I spend my time, and how I'm treated. Kids don't have that same luxury. On one hand, we ask them to advocate for themselves and have a growth mindset, but the environments provided for them don't always allow them to do so. How counterproductive. We're setting these kids up with the hope they can make a better day for themselves, only to find it doesn't work.

Is this their bright future? And we wonder why they're anxious. It's upsetting to be sold a message of freedom, only to still be found in chains. Since we can't often give children the freedom we have, we must provide better environments for them. It's not necessarily more freedom our children need, it's more adults waking up to creating better realities for our kids.

I'm not one to helicopter my kids. You can ask them. I believe strongly in perseverance through hard things and often parent them through the phrase, "Life's hard, but you gotta do it anyway," but I promised myself after my son was suicidal at eight years old that he would always have a choice over his environment. The reason many young people are depressed is that aspects of their various environments are making them sad and they feel no power or control to change it.

My son will always have a choice. If school is a source of crippling anxiety, then I'll let him choose how he would like to be schooled. The end goal is a Grade Twelve education; he gets a say in how he gets there. My son had a choice to make regarding school. Every day, he would complain about school, so I reminded him, "Son, you always have a choice of what your reality looks like. Own your decision to either face school with courage or homeschool."

When I first started homeschooling my son, nothing got done. It was a challenge for me, as I like checking off the tasks, but I had to remember that the lesson doesn't exist to get done, it exists to empower the student. Some days, my son didn't have the mental or emotional capacity and he needed to rest. Sometimes that was for a few minutes, sometimes it was for a few hours. I thought about it; if my son had an illness like cancer, I would instantly understand the need to rest. Isn't that the same for a mind that needs healing?

After a few months of taking it slow, he started becoming more alive. As I went with his pace, he started to be able to handle a little more each day. A few months later, he was back to being curious and self-motivated. Our natural state is curious. Humans love to learn. We're always learning. Traditional school for my son took *away* his desire to learn. When my son has control over what he's learning and he's free to explore his own curiosity, no one can stop him from learning. We still do what is expected for math, but all other subjects are led by what he wants to learn. I see no signs of anxiety when we school this way.

Anxiety doesn't always look like "fear;" it can also show up in our kids as aggression or overreacting. One time, my son didn't want to go to school so I decided he needed some tough love. I explained to him that he could either push through and go to school or he could stay home, but no screens for the weekend. There was crying, an Emmy-worthy performance of fainting, and telling me what a horrible mother I was for "making him" go to school. I then reminded him that his decision was his and his alone to make. I gave him a choice, and asked him to *own* his choice. Anxiety for my son was a rollercoaster of dramatic emotion, blame, yelling, and making strange demands. I was exhausted from the pushback that day.

We as parents have to be willing to make the hard decisions that will hopefully not allow anxiety to rule our children's hearts. We have to remember to stand firm and remember whom we are forming our children to be one year—or even ten years—from now. It's worth the temporal discomfort. Kids, such as my son, who struggle with anxiety can literally feel physically sick. It's a tough one to navigate.

If you're a parent of a child struggling with anxiety, it's important to give your children the structure and strength they need in order to become overcomers. This might not always mean we're giving them what they want in the moment, but we can affirm that nothing will break our connection with them.

There have been more times to count when I would have to cancel coffee dates, special outings, and even work because my son was having an anxiety attack or meltdown. One thing I've had to do for the many years with my son's mental health challenges is to be flexible to postpone or reschedule fun outings in order to be present and to refuel after the emotional exhaustion. Children suffering from a moment of anxiety need us present to help them feel safe through their storms. After the anxiety subsides, they need us to help them recover by talking with them through the situation. They need to know everything is going to be okay. This isn't a one-time thing. They need us to do this repeatedly until their brain learns to regulate. The time we take to do this is vital. If we don't, we only push them further into anxiety. Anxiety grows in isolation. I believe the reason so many young people are struggling with anxiety is because of the lack of adults in their lives to walk them through this.

You might wonder if, in doing this, you're "babying" your child, but I assure you that your presence with them is working wonders in their favour. Sometimes they need a hug and assurance; other times, they need some tough love, but not without us reminding them that we're with them through it. Use connection and empathy, and observe how your child responds. "Feel out" every situation. You'll know if your tough love is pushing them over the edge. When your child feels held by you, they often can push through things they never thought they could, but their cup needs to be full first. If their cup is empty, avoid pushing them until you've filled it with the connection and love they need. You're not being permissive or weak, you're doing what's needed before they can move forward.

As much as missing out on coffee dates and work has been disappointing and sometimes straight-up inconvenient, I realize that I have only my son for a short season of his life and I need to do all I can to set him up for success. I have many years of coffee dates and work ahead of me; for now, my son is my priority. I am the adult in his life.

Youth today are struggling because we're trying to parent them the way we were parented. "Suck it up" only works when they feel understood, supported, nurtured, and connected to their caregivers. They're not weak or pathetic if they can't do simple tasks. Anxiety is an alarm. It tells us a story about how they are doing on the inside. They don't have the prefrontal cortex to reason and use words to help us understand their deep emotions. They can't always process what's going on inside of them. Teens are going through a brain overhaul and a flood of hormones. They need us beside them to help them through these turbulent waters.

The issues youth and children face today are different from when we were kids. Yes, anxiety and depression have always been there, but the environmental factors kids face today only enhances them greatly. We didn't have social media screaming our inadequacies at us. We didn't hear of wars and school shootings. We didn't have a lot of choice for many things. There were a couple of TV channels and only select times when cartoons would play. Today's culture has only increased anxiety for our children.

Youth and people everywhere are saying the same thing. They don't want to feel judged. They want to belong and be understood. Do we know how to create a culture of belonging? What happens to mental illness when people feel supported, understood, and not judged? Anxiety doesn't rule in a space like that.

In order to combat anxiety, we need to notice where shame is. My son would often say to me, "Stop shaming me, Mom!" I didn't realize how often I would do this. I'm glad he noticed when he felt shame and was able to communicate it. Naming it is the first step to bringing it to the light so that it loses its power. The times I would shame my son the most was when *I* felt the most shame. Whether it was after dinner at my parents' house, where my approach to his mental health was questioned, to being embarrassed by his behaviour in public, to his poor decisions at school, I would shame him most when I felt shamed. Noticing this pattern was key for me to stop allowing the opinions of others to dictate how I felt about myself and how I parented my son.

Shame causes us to become the opposite of what we desire. Being shamed only pushes us downwards. We thrive with safe connections, both physically and emotionally. There's nothing worse than experiencing the sting of once feeling like you belong to being pushed away, betrayed, or forgotten. The internal confusion of this creates is where shame is born. However, when we experience authentic belonging, we become strong.

I kept a shame journal for a short time. Every time I had a thought in my day that resonated, "I am not enough," I wrote it down. It was a shocking process. One morning I had ten statements before ten o'clock in the morning! These thoughts were swimming around in my subconscious, dictating my mood, psychical demeanour, and soul temperature. But shame exposed loses its power.

What are the shame statements you believe about yourself?

What are the shame statements you believe about your child? What about their behaviours? Their habits?

Here are some practical tips to help your child with their anxiety from this chapter.

- Look for what's underneath anxiety. Anxiety is always accompanied.
- Be careful not to judge your child for the things they can't do because of anxiety. This will only increase it.
- Fill their cup with connection with you before you seek to push them through challenges that overwhelm them.
- Give them a choice over their environments when you can. It's not always possible to homeschool. If school is causing anxiety, see what you can do to help them cope with the class they are in or find a school that's more suitable.
- Remind them of their power. Remind them of what they have control over: themselves, the friends they choose, etc. Brainstorm what they do have control over, to help them feel empowered.

- Notice your shame triggers and how it affects your interactions with your family.
- Create an environment of belonging in your home, where your child feels seen and understood.
- Be flexible with your schedule. You will need to cancel coffee dates, etc. It's just the way it is. Find work that can understand your situation with your child that gives flexibility to possibly work from home so you can be ready to respond rather than react when anxiety hits. It never happens at a convenient time.

You don't control your kids, but as you can see from this chapter, there's a lot that you do have control over. Control yourself first, apply the tools given, and you will see as you practice these over the long haul that a new story is written for your children. Don't expect a new kid by Friday. Make it your intention to incorporate these tools as a lifestyle and be committed for the long haul.

That's where the magic happens.

Chapter Ten

You Are Your Child's Dope

MANY PARENTS ARE CONCERNED ABOUT THE POTENTIAL ADDICTIONS LURKING AT THEIR child's door. Many youths are turning to cannabis to ease their social anxiety and other issues, such as ADHD. Some children would spend hours on video games if they could. How do we deal with this as parents? Parents want to know what the solutions are in our addictive culture. We will explore some answers in this chapter.

When it comes to conversations with youth around cannabis, I don't centre on the *what* (what's right or wrong with it), but the *why*. "Why do you feel you need it? Is it to calm nerves? Social anxiety? Anxiety? Depression?" Focusing on the why allows us to get to issues underneath behaviour to focus on the root, which is many times shame.

"I don't feel like I can be myself without it."

"I don't have what it takes to make it through school."

"It helps me get through the day."

What these youth are really looking for is *belonging*. When they have that, cannabis loses its lustre.

You are your child's dope. Home should be the number-one place our children feel is their safe refuge. This alone could significantly decrease any addiction.

Youth today aren't feeling there is a lot of hope out there. When I asked a Grade Nine class to tell me what they're noticing around mental health, one of the students said this, "There's not one day that goes by at school when I don't hear someone say they want to die."

Everyone nodded their heads.

Another student added, "Everyone is always just… sad."

My own son has said to me numerous times, "I don't see a lot of hope for the future." More than ever, youth need to be reconnected back to hope for their present and future.

When I was a young person, we were constantly being told we could make a difference in our world, that our lives mattered. Gen-Xers were told we were "special." There are both pros and cons to this, of course, but the pro is that it created a generation that would challenge the status quo of previous generations. We didn't want to work the same job our entire lives. We started to explore entrepreneurship. We were told our future was bright and we were ready to face it. Our proceeding millennial generation has continued to push the limits even further.

However, these young ones, born 2000 to present, are different. They've lost that same fire and sense of purpose. What happened?

My son said to me, "Mom, all there is to life is going to school, work, and then retiring. What kind of life is that?" Where does he get this idea from? Certainly not from our entrepreneurial home. My son often tells me I live in the land of unicorns and rainbows. I sure do! If you tell me the future is bright, not only will I believe you, but I'll do my part to make it happen.

Today's youth struggling with addictions have become disconnected from a hopeful future. High school students are stressed about marks and university entrance.

"What if I can't get into college?"

"What if I can't find a job?"

"What if I can't keep a job?"

Some can't even picture where they will be in a few months—let alone a few years. I saw this quote on a youth's social media: "I am trying to live a life I don't understand."

We tell youth to make a difference—to develop solutions to the issues we see around us. The problem is that many young people see today's problems as insurmountable. My son once said to me, "Mom, I don't want to change the world. I really don't care."

Where does this apathy stem from? I believe it comes from being overwhelmed with the tsunami of emotions and mental barriers in his own mind topped with having no idea if what he would do would even make a difference. Youth today are bombarded with YouTube stars and Instagram heroes. The message this potentially sends to youth is: "Go big or go home." If you're not an instant YouTube sensation, then what's the point? If you don't have 1K followers with a bunch of likes, then who are you to make a difference?

Issues of bullying and suicide are prominent among today's youth, and it's not just in high schools. Kids as young as age seven or eight are experiencing bullying and even thoughts of suicide. Remember, my son was only eight years old when he was verbally suicidal. Video games offer an escape from the real world when it's just too hard. Shame tells our kids, "You don't have what it takes to face the real world." Social anxiety is rising among our youth, offering weed as a remedy to help them cope. Some students have confessed to me they smoke three joints at school just to be able to make it through their day.

I've noticed a switch in youth in the last few years regarding connection. They don't seem to know how to connect with others. They show up to school with their armour on, scared to trust. They bury themselves under a label of "social anxiety." The work I have done in schools is holy work. Through movement and work done in a circle, I help them discover that joy, laughter, fun, and creativity happen when we let our armour down to connect. It's truly beautiful when students begin to get it. You can see them come alive when they realize everyone feels just like they do: scared, insecure, and uncertain. When belonging is created, social anxiety had no place. What we need to do is teach our children how to connect again. The problem is that many of us don't know how to connect any longer, as well. It's easier to scroll through social media for updates. We communicate through text. Our schedules are so busy we have to schedule playdates weeks in advance.

I asked my Facebook friends what they thought was hindering connection today. Here are some of the comments made:
- distracted parents
- we spend more time checking our phones than checking our children
- working full time and sometimes two to three jobs
- no mealtimes together
- unrealistic expectations of ourselves
- mommy guilt
- busyness
- social media
- society's too quick-based

- our unrealistic expectations
- when we choose to just get by, when surviving is enough
- filling up our children's schedules with extracurricular activities
- our own lack of knowledge and limitations
- children wanting to do other things other than being with us
- our own baggage
- no time for meaningful conversations
- really listening to our kids and being willing to really hear them out

This is not okay. I'm calling the adults back to the game to create something better for our kids. Connection is needed more than ever for our youth. We must teach and model for them what that looks like.

In a conversation with my oldest about patterns of parenting being passed down from generation to generation, he said this: "Be the parent you wanted your parents to be."

Wow. Mic drop.

Dope, the old slang word for marijuana, comes from the word "dopamine," which is the key chemical in the mind involved in addiction. All addictions seek to appease it. Dopamine is about feeling the reward of stimulating what a dysregulated mind is missing: connection. Substances don't require social skills. These "substances" that increase the dopamine in the mind don't have to be drugs or alcohol; they can be anything we're attached to that gives us that "fix"—such as shopping, eating, sugar, sex, extreme sports, Instagram likes, and video games.

All of these activate the same chemical dope that drug and alcohol addictions do. And the more you fill the brain's chemicals need with your substance of choice, the more it will need next time to get that fix of dopamine released in the mind.

What's even more intense is that the dopamine release acts even before the partaking of the substance. It's aroused even with familiar sights and smells that signal to the brain that your drug is near. And we wonder why it's so hard to quit? That chemical wants to be satisfied and is literally playing with your mind until you get it.

It's not about what your drug is; it's about the dope you seek to fill what's lacking in your environment. And so the cycle repeats. Let's break it down:

Your environment shapes your brain. Perhaps the environment you are in doesn't provide the connection you need.

A substance offers you the dopamine fix you seek.

Unfortunately, instead of feeling connected, you sink further into isolation and into the substance.

The counterfeit you consume promises the feeling of connection does not deliver and is now damaging your decision-making abilities and creating more dysregulation in your mind.

You need more dope, more substance.

Round and round you go.

See how it's not as easy as just going into rehab, or vowing to quit? We're not addicted to substances; rather, we're addicted to the brain chemical dopamine, and it's a ruthless one.

The mistake many parents are making is assuming that putting our children in bubble wrap is going to prevent anything bad from happening to them. Helicopter parenting looks like being our children's dope, but it's counterfeit. It's creating more anxiety than we know.

We need grounded confidence as parents. We need to allow our children to explore, learn, express their curiosity and creativity, and—the big one—make mistakes and learn from them. It's a fine line between the bubble wrap and letting our kids destroy themselves and the world around them. Many of us wrestle with this, wondering if we're making the right decision to let our children adventure off when all we want to do is hold them tight and never let them go. When we struggle with the challenges our children experience, it's our job to show them the road to overcoming.

The key to this dance is to keep connection at the forefront—always. When your child is stepping out to risk, remind them you are there. Confident, strong kids are those who know their parents have their back, no matter what the outcome. They know that when they make poor decisions, they won't be shamed, but they will have someone safe to walk through the journey with them.

The youth I've seen in jail and at-risk programs are the ones who had to go it all alone on their journey. I often wonder how different their lives would look if they had someone safe to connect and journey with them.

However, all is not lost. If a healthy environment created by a loving connection can cause the brain to be regulated, then you and I have a powerful tool. If we're willing to work on the environments we're creating for our children, then there's hope for us to be the dope our children need.

You are your child's dope.

Just like substances release dopamine in the mind, so does a loving parent look into the eyes of their child. It's all we all need—to feel the warm effects of belonging to appease the brain chemical in the way it was meant to be satisfied. This keeps addiction at bay. Supportive friendships and healthy communities are the real dope we long for. When we provide that for one another, social issues like addiction don't stand a chance.

We now come to the part of the chapter many of you are waiting for.

"But what about screens and devices? They're the problem, I tell you!"

I personally don't believe screens are the enemy. I think we need to be much more concerned with the amount of screen time we're using as adults than our children. If we want our children to put down their phones, we should go first. Phones have taken over our lives. We can be contacted anytime, anywhere and they often interrupt meaningful moments.

I'm the first one guilty of this. How many times was I on my phone while my youngest played at the play place? To me, it was a time to get work done or unwind. Little did I know, he was watching me. When I'm on my devices all the time with my children around, they will just assume this is the way life is. Then they wonder why we're asking them to get off theirs. Many parents don't like it when I say this, but the first person who needs a screen check is you. Set the example.

The way I handle screens with my boys is to help manage the freedom these devices require. We can't guard our children forever against the waves of information and sometimes-sketchy material they'll encounter with one click of a button. It's always been my desire to teach my sons how to navigate through this while encouraging the value of guarding their hearts above all else to be the filter through which they decide what's permissible and what should be avoided.

This isn't easy. It would be much easier to allow children to watch and play whatever they want or take screens away altogether than to teach them how to manage screens. It's all hands on deck, with time and dedication on the part of the parent.

Limiting screen time isn't even the issue. With the debut of the iPhone and iPad, etc., there hasn't been substantial research about how increased screens have affected young minds. The good news is that research is starting to evolve. The bad news is that it's not looking good, and our job as parents to help our children navigate just became more difficult. I always say to my boys that I will not limit their screen time until I see a need for limitation.

For example, when I ask for them to get off and they argue, *that's* when I have a problem with it. When the suggestion of bike rides and walks together become "lame," that sends a red flag. When friends come over and all the kids come to us parents with sullen faces and proclamations, "We're bored without video games," then its clear screens have become an issue.

One year, these very issues had increased in our home. So we decided to take that entire summer off of all screens. It was hard at times, as you might imagine, but we spent more time together, laughed more, and found needed rest for our minds that summer.

Our children have become overstimulated and unable to process the delay of gratification because of screens. The problem with video games, multitasking, and constant iPad use is that this type of activity releases dopamine. When you're used to the high arousal state screens constantly provide, it's hard to see something like nature as fascinating. The dopamine needs to be fed and at higher levels each time. Video game creators are constantly levelling up video game stimulation by creating visuals that are faster and more complex, increasing the intensity in rewards, which then increases the adrenaline experienced.

How can a bike ride or hike compete? It pales in comparison.

Research has started to show how screen use affected the central nervous system. It puts the body into a state of constant arousal, followed by a crash. Think about it. Does your child experience mood swings? Concentration problems? Limited interests outside of wanting to stay in front of the computer? Other side-effects of overuse of screens are: depression, inability to handle frustration, poor sportsmanship, unable to handle emotions, social immaturity, insomnia, and keeping eye contact.

This is what coming down from dopamine overload looks like. Dopamine demands more; it becomes an addiction to arousal. Does that sound like children today? Curiosity dies when it's replaced with a dependency on screens to escape the nemesis called boredom.

Sometimes the loss of screens can cause anxiety. Screens have become a form of self-medication. I know this became true for my oldest son. Screen time overkill (much like what it's like around my home in the middle of a cold Canadian winter) puts a child in a state of chronic stress due to the part of the brain activated in active screen time. Screens bypass the prefrontal cortex, where empathy and creativity are formed, and utilize the fight-or-flight part of the brain.

Using this part of the brain continually will put our body in a state of chronic stress. No wonder students are more stressed out and anxious than ever. They never get a breather. Chronic stress leads to dysregulation—the ability to modulate responses appropriate for the surroundings present. Ever seen a child locked in defensive mode? It's survival mode, trained by constantly living in the fight-or-flight part of the brain. This then increases the cortisol hormone, which affects blood sugar levels. Children with attachment to screens often crave sweets too. This type of stress affects a child's ability to sort new facts and retain new information. You could accurately say it increases the appearance of what looks like ADHD.

When my oldest started to protest leaving the house due to missing out on his favourite game, I knew we needed a change. When I realized that we'd been handing our youngest screens to entertain himself during the year we were dealing with our oldest's depression and anxiety, he experienced a negative change. We observed anger, aggression, and a decrease in motivation.

It was truly sobering to look at the negative patterns created by my permissiveness. But there's also hope because we have the power to create boundaries and paths to resilience for our children that can help them manage the world of screens.

The goal of our screen-free summer was to give my children's nervous systems a break and see some of the negative attachments and behaviours disappear. My husband and I also noticed what screen overload was doing to us. Make no mistake, adults are affected too.

Here's a handy summary for you that summarizes the main ways in which screens affect children (and adults):

1. Immediate gratification
2. Video games keep the gamer engaged by giving them a sense of control and choices, which leads to instant rewards (immediate gratification). Instant rewards increase dopamine levels, the feel-good chemical in the brain, through the roof. The problem with feeding reward systems and dopamine in the mind is that it takes more and more to appease it. Research is finding in children the same reward circuits that are being activated with video games are the same reward circuits that feed harmful addictions.
3. The other problem with raising dopamine levels through the fast-paced rewards that are given through video games is that it puts the body into a high state of arousal, followed by a crash. This is where we see our children become dysregulated, moody, anxious, and sometimes aggressive. Dopamine is what makes the player want to play more. Game designers are geniuses at creating intensity in their games to satisfy the inner reward system. Coming down from high dopamine levels causes a child to become disorganized and/or anxious. The other problem is that

serotonin—which is important for being social, having a stable mood, and coping with stress—becomes more dysregulated with video game play, making games seem more like self-medication.

4. Stress

5. The hyperarousal that video games create is caused by the constant state of being in "fight-or-flight brain," making it hard to relax or think things through. When a child constantly lives in their fight-or-flight brain, it becomes hard to regulate. The nervous system is in a state of stress, and if that's prolonged, it can actually cause damage. If you've ever experienced a time when your child, who is normally fairly even-tempered, turn almost savage after being asked to stop playing a game, it's because their nervous system is overloaded.

6. Loss of curiosity

7. To be human is to be curious, inspiring creativity. Unfortunately, slow-cooked creativity that comes from a curiosity about life can't compete with the high levels of dopamine release a video game can provide. Normal things become boring. Nature is too slow. Relationships become too much effort for too much pain compared to the instant gratification rewards that a game offers. There's simply no comparison.

We need to pause for a moment. Remember that mantra we created at the beginning of the book? This is still a no-shame zone. It's hard to read the reality of what happens with too much screen time and video game stimulation, isn't it?

Remember, these are just facts to keep in mind. Please don't allow shame to turn you into what my kids call me—"The Screen Police." I used to research the effects of screen time, immediately panic, then turn into Sergeant Anti-Screen, instead of taking time to carefully watch my boys with screens and have a conversation about my observations. This is what I do now, and it works much better than, "That's it! No more screens for you!" We lose an opportunity to allow our children to observe how screens are making them feel and make healthy choices with our guidance.

Interestingly enough, when we were about a month and a half through our screen-free summer, I noticed how much my boys actually needed games for downtime. When I allowed the boys to play for a limited time near the end of the summer, I recognized that it actually refreshed them. At that moment, I realized that it was going to take time and great intention on my part to navigate the waters of balancing screens in our home.

Coming back into the fall and permission again for screens, my goal was to train my boys to learn how to handle them. For example, my youngest can't handle the same amount of time on a screen as my oldest without becoming moody and dysregulated. I'm teaching him to notice the signs and get off the screen before it gets out of control. As for what my boys really thought about this process, they will tell you it was horrible, but deep inside it has built the awareness inside of them that screens can easily get out of control. We all noticed the difference in our mood over the summer (but they won't tell you that).

When it comes to screens, I believe we need to keep the conversation open with our children and centre it not on how much *time* they should have on it, but rather on these three things:

GUARD YOUR HEART

I ask my children often, "How is this game affecting your heart? What do you notice about your attitude or behaviour after playing it?" I ask the same with YouTube videos. I want to teach my children to think about how games and videos affect them, rather than me timing them or using an app that turns off all screens at a certain time. What are they noticing? At first, my children didn't notice anything. They didn't care; they just wanted to play. But as I have consistently asked this question now over the years, I've watched them become more aware.

For example, my youngest loves retro games. I noticed after he would play Street Fighter, he would become more aggressive. I talked to him about this, and noticed the next time he went to play the game, he quit the game after five minutes and hasn't played it since.

We can help our children begin to notice for themselves how screens are affecting them so they can begin to make positive decisions for themselves. There has been an enormous difference in my boys since I've made the switch from "barking" about how much screen time they have had to focus on their heart.

THE RESPONSIBILITY OF SCREENS

To me, navigating screens is no different from the responsibility needed to drive a car. We wouldn't hand our five-year-old the keys to our car and we certainly wouldn't hand the keys to our sixteen-year-old without them taking a test to assure us they will drive responsibly.

I believe the same for navigating screens. We need to talk to our kids about the level of responsibility screens require. The limits we set for a five-year-old will be much different for those of a sixteen-year-old. Are they navigating screens wisely? With the introduction of the iPad and smartphones, we handed our children over to this new world rather quickly, not realizing what the potential impact could be.

Now that we are further along and we see the effects screens have on children and youth, we need to avoid simply handing our children over to the screen to entertain them, but rather educate them on how to be responsible with screens. This includes searching and researching on the Internet, how to stay safe, cyberbullying, social media, etc., but also how much time they should spend on screens, and how to guard their hearts.

YOUR EXPECTATIONS REGARDING SCREENS

Have you been clear on your expectations regarding screens? Have you created a structure for your children around them?

For example, in my home, we keep our screens in the living room. I'm also clear about YouTube videos and memes that are not allowed to be watched because of content. When my oldest joined Instagram, I was very clear about my expectations around its proper use and online bullying. One day, my oldest was telling me about a group chat his class had on Instagram that was making fun of one of the girls in school. I reminded him that this was not the proper use of the app, and that he had a choice: either leave the group chat or lose the phone.

Whatever your expectations are around screens, make sure you have communicated these to your children. Think your expectations through and avoid creating random rules out of nowhere.

There have been a few times when I've had to intervene and remove my children's devices from them. I do this when they're not using them responsibly, or I'm noticing negative patterns in their behaviour that they aren't noticing themselves.

You have every right to take away screens when they're not being used responsibly. My advice here? Don't just take the screens away and leave it at that; rather, talk to your child first about what you've noticed and see if they notice it too.

I've surprised my children at school by taking their screens away right there. As you can imagine, it backfired on me. Instead of them thinking about how to use their screens more wisely, all they could think about was how ridiculous I was.

When we talk to our children about what I'm noticing and asking them if they're noticing it too, we engage in eye-opening conversations that are shaping the way they navigate screens for themselves.

No guilt needed. There's no "right" answer. Every child is different. You can teach your children to be masters of the screen, rather than the other way around. What's at the centre of all addictions is, once again, *connection*. With us by our children's side, we can help them navigate screens and addictions. You're not just a parent; you're preventing addiction. You're a culture maker.

With connection at the centre, our children will discover a hopeful future again because they will have a secure base from which to navigate life.

Chapter Eleven
Belonging Creates Resilience

"Belonging is the message of this decade."
(Paul Born, source unknown)

I REMEMBER DOING AN EXERCISE WITH A GROUP OF SEVENTH-GRADERS AT A SCHOOL. We had the students write down every label they had been given that year. One seventh-grade boy wrote down seven cruel labels he had been given that year alone. It was heartbreaking. We then had students flip the page over, pass their sheets around, and had the other students in the class write down the positive things they saw in one another.

When the seventh-grade boy received his sheet, his eyes filled with tears. He said, "I've never had such nice things said about me!"

Our children often leave the house, only to have horrible things spoken to them at school by peers. Home needs to be a refuge where life is spoken. Instead of saying, "What's wrong with you?" we could ask, "What happened to you?"

When my son was continually getting sent to the principal's office daily, I didn't react; I simply asked him, "What's going on, son?" Children are constantly being told stories of what they are *not*. They need to come home and hear everything that they *are*. Home needs to be a place of emotional safety and empowerment to see resilient children.

Think about you can you encourage your child today.

Once, when my son became upset about his diagnosis of anxiety, depression, ADHD, and ODD, he yelled, "I'm so stupid I have nothing! I feel like an idiot!"

I sat him down and replied, "Son, don't ever let anything limit you. You are limitless. There is no diagnosis that can tell you who you are."

Diagnoses are helpful to know how to help our children, but they can become problematic when we let them define us. More than ever, speak life into your kids.

They'll say it's weird. They may brush it off, but you better believe they love it, even though they will never let you know.

What creates belonging? Belonging has to be felt. Being understood creates belonging. You can put beautiful décor that states, "Everyone Belongs in This Home" on your walls, but until your children feel it, it doesn't count. One of the greatest ways to create belonging by seeking to understand instead of seeking to be understood.

In a 1995–1997 study from Kaiser Permanente[2] in San Diego on the Adverse Childhood Experience (ACE) questionnaire, of all the terrible things that could happen to a child or youth, *emotional* abuse was more likely to cause depression more than any other kind of abuse.

How we speak to our kids matters. We sometimes forget how powerful our nonverbal communication is to our children. Nonverbal communication creates the feeling of belonging. Kids have incredible "spidey-senses." They know when we think they're an inconvenience to us.

You have the power to be your child's battle or victory. Creating belonging in our homes is crucial.

I remember my son telling me he felt homesick. He said this not only once, but a few times. The thing is, he said this *while* he was home. I've heard other young people say the same thing to me.

I wondered what this meant until I discovered that it's a longing for deep and meaningful connection that they know they're meant for. It's a cry to feel rooted and nurtured. We need to give that to them. Let's put down the phone, create work boundaries, stop the distractions, and connect and enjoy our children.

Belonging is not a tool. Everyone wants "tools" today. More strategies. You've already got the tools and strategies inside of you. As a wonderfully created human being, you are wired to connect with your children. You can bring a home filled with belonging and rest when you discover for yourself that you *belong*. You create belonging by experiencing belonging for yourself first.

I remember when my two sons were being horrible to each other with their words. It was having a deep impact on both of them, so I made cartoon pictures

---

[2] https://www.cdc.gov/violenceprevention/childabuseandneglect/acestudy/about.html

of both of them and put them on the fridge. These were not wonderful cartoon drawings—rather, they were the drawings of a second-grade child, but it would have to do.

Every time they spoke a cruel word to one another, I taped that word onto their cartoon body. By the end of the day, I was able to show them the number of words they spoke to one another. We were able to talk about how these words made them feel. The visual really brought it home to them. They didn't realize how they let their tongues run wild. We started a new challenge of putting kind words onto the cartoon characters and talked about the difference they felt in their hearts when they did so.

Teaching my children empathy and compassion is first my job, which is then enhanced by our attachment village of teachers and adults.

Our words *create*.

While teaching a group of sixth-graders, there was one boy who was labelled by his whole class "the bully." I looked over at the teacher, who also nodded her head in agreement. I pushed through the discomfort of how this boy must have felt to use it at an opportunity for the class to learn that labels create destinies. Label someone a "bully" and they have nothing to rise to other than that.

But what if we could see past the outside behaviour and truly see the person inside? So that's what we did. We took a moment to bring this boy to the middle of the circle. The students were challenged to see him and call out the gold they saw inside of him. After taking a moment, they spoke the most thoughtful, sincere words that surprised him. It wasn't just the boy who was affected by that exercise, it was also the class.

They were reminded again that words create. They experienced firsthand what it's like to lay down our idea of others to really see them and the life it can create. Words can bring to life or they can create emptiness, pain, and despair. People will always live up to our expectations—positive or negative. When people don't feel they belong they become the worst versions of themselves.

I'm convinced that if teachers took a few moments out of each week or day to practise this, we would see more cultures of belonging and less bullying and anxiety in our schools. Youth and children today deserve and have a legitimate need to feel valuable every day. We need a revolution in empathy. We can write about how we are "bully-free" or "free from racism," but if people don't feel it, it doesn't count.

I'm calling out for braver conversations about what's hindering inclusion. We need to be courageous to face what hinders belonging. We all want our homes, schools, and places of work to experience it, but it's a whole other level to look at the barriers r why people aren't experiencing it. If we can be vulnerable enough to name and face the barriers, we can see our places become free of bullying, racism, indifference, and exclusion.

Someone mentioned this to me this week: "There's a difference between an environment that embraces people and one that is free of shame." It's possible to embrace people and still shame them.

The greatest barrier to belonging is that we're not willing to lay ourselves down for one another. You read that right. Belonging is not something you fight for or hold with a closed fist. When you truly know you belong, you can extend belonging to others, which includes an open hand. This means that instead of fighting for my rights, I lay them down. This means instead of stripping you of your rights so I can have mine, I come to a table where all are given seats of honour and we treat one another likewise.

Last year, I produced a theatre show in my city called "Rewritten." I took nine dance and spoken word artists through a process of discovering what experiences, words, people, and environments formed the person they are today. I did not expect what a profound process this would become. The artists dove into hard topics, such as the "Me Too Movement," sexuality, racism, colonialism, and relationships. Each person told their story from behind a life-sized wooden frame.

At the end of the show, each artist lowered their frame to the stage floor to symbolize the idea of laying down our framework, the way we view the world through our experiences, to be able to see others. We had given each audience member a small popsicle frame when they arrived. At the end of the show, one inspired audience member threw their frame on to the stage.

Suddenly, there were hundreds of wooden frames flying through the air on to the stage floor to symbolize each person wanting to learn to lay down their framework, as well.

This was one of the most profound moments I've ever experienced in my artistic career. It reminded me, yet again, that we as humans all want the same thing. We want to lay down ourselves to see others, but it's the *actual doing it* that's so hard.

I've decided my next theatre production is going to start where that show finished, with the frames on the floor and answering the question, "Now what?" How do we lay ourselves down? What does connection look like through the eyes of a woman who has experienced rape? How does reconciliation really happen where we no longer see the polarization we experience today? It's a tough one, but these are the conversations around belonging I know are worth the risk.

I remember when I was touring a show with a group of young adults. We were empowering young people to create a better world around them. I walked into the green room before the show to hear them singing, "I hate people, I hate people." The truth is, people suck. You're having a great day and then "people happen." People bring out our heart wounds. A heart wound makes it so that instead of speaking life to someone else, we speak from our wounds. It is Yet it's good to notice these heart wounds.

Another barrier to belonging is not listening to one another. Instead of thinking of your next statement, or looking to see who else is in the room, what if we focused our attention on who we're conversing with, seeking to see the world through their eyes. When we read between their words, we hear what they are really crying out for—to be heard, to be understood, to be embraced. This is what everyone longs for.

One of our greatest needs is to feel understood and accepted. There's a saying, "hurt people hurt people." This is completely true. It's also true that people who are not understood can't understand themselves, and then have no capacity to understand others. People who aren't heard can't hear others. People who are shamed will shame others. Our temptation is to be offended and put up walls, rather than being broken for one another and humble ourselves to reconnect. We get too occupied with our own hurts, our own desire to be understood, rather than to understand. This is a real sacrifice. If we preach community, then we have to be willing to do the hard stuff to live it. Community means looking into the face of one another and not running away. It's choosing to stay in the grit until we get through it together.

Community is messy.

I recently experienced a rupture in a close friendship. Feelings were hurt. We both were deeply affected. I was angry. I felt my friend was overreacting. She didn't feel heard. After a few days of calming my heart down and gaining perspective, I reached out to her and said, "This has been hard, but I'm keeping connection with you my number-one goal. You matter to me. If our friendship survives this, *that* is the win."

The friendship survival had to be the win, not proving my point, not being right or vindicated. My friend mattered to me. That's what was most important. It's easy to say that now, looking back, but in the moment, it was hard.

What my son said when he was eight sums it up perfectly: "When I'm angry, people look different." I was angry, and I had to remind myself that my friend was not my enemy. I had to take some time and gain perspective in order to come to the point when I could lay myself down. The rupture in our relationship took a few months of consistently being brave as issues came up. One brave conversation wasn't going to repair our friendship. It took many.

When I thought all was said and done, I received another email from my friend. I was tired of hearing the same old, same old. I was frustrated we weren't over this. But as I laid my own thoughts down and really looked at her words, I saw she was in need. My job was to figure out what that was.

Then it hit me—I hadn't asked her to forgive me for how I made her feel. We are taught in our culture to speak our own truth and tell everyone who doesn't understand to "screw off." If you want connection, this can't be your mantra. Healthy boundaries are important (and we'll get to that in the next few chapters), but if you want to learn how to handle conflict well, you're going to need to learn the art of asking for forgiveness and learn how to give it. After I asked for forgiveness, the issue was done. I can say with confidence that we overcame something that could have completely destroyed our relationship.

We have the ability to bring refreshment to others.

Connection is key.

Belonging and connection are important to create not only in our homes, but also in our lives with other relationships. Connection comes from deep within us. It's who we *are*, not what we *do*. Connection means we value relationships above everything else. It looks like this:

I will lay down my need to be important.

I will lay down my need to be right.

I will see the world through your eyes for a moment so I can connect with you.

The more we practice this with the relationships in our lives, the more it becomes part of us. We become more compassionate.

We need to be able to see past people's prickles. I have watched my son struggle with relationships because at times his peers and their parents haven't been able to see past his quirks and prickles. He hasn't been "cool enough" for some, not "well behaved enough" for others, so what does he do? He retreats further into his games, where he can imagine a world in which he fits just perfectly. The problem with children like my son is that the one thing they need to bring them to life—positive relationships—seems to be the one thing they can never get.

In order to create a sense of belonging, we have to break the rules. Society tells us to judge and question the "other." We must rebel and become the supportive, face-to-face community that says, "I might not completely understand, but I'm *for* you, I believe in you, and we are we're going to make sure you get through this."

"No one left behind" must be our mandate. When people are affirmed by a safe community of people, there's no stopping the creativity, problem-solving, and innovation that can follow. The goal of an empowering community is that we all get to cross the finish line *together*. Community is only as strong as the belonging we create for all. There's great resilience where there's belonging.

A self-centred existence leads us with a life without purpose. I've always wondered if the quest for self-fulfillment is ever quenched. My friend just arrived back from a trip to California, where he spent a day with a millionaire who stated he hadn't had a meaningful connection with another human in a few months. He explained to me how lonely the rich man was and how refreshed he was after a meaningful time with someone else. Too many find themselves without authentic friendships or safe family relationships. At the same time, culture sells us a message of making something of yourself. We fall for it because there's really no one else to look to anyway.

We're in desperate need of attachment villages. Who has that today? Very few of us. For many, the idea of an attachment village is obsolete.

It grieves me that my children are not growing up the way I did. We're fortunate to know our neighbours beside us, but as for having consistent community, it's been challenging. The city we live in is a city of hustle. Arranging coffees or playdates are often needing to be scheduled weeks ahead of time. It's exhausting trying to get together with people.

My mom is in Arizona for six months of the year, and my husband's parents are ten hours away. Finding childcare has been extremely challenging and disappointing. This is one of the reasons that I decided to leave the regular workforce and become an entrepreneur. My children's mental wellness requires this. My children don't like going to strangers' homes to be looked after. They aren't even all that fond of people we know.

This is our reality. I'm not going to lie; it has often felt very lonely and isolating. I wish my sons could experience the endless play I experienced right out my front door with all the neighbourhood kids. My grandparents were the best caregivers I could have asked for. I wasn't a latchkey kid. I had roots to come home to. I felt both surrounded and secure.

Youth today aren't as connected with adults in the same way I was when I was a youth. At church, I could never leave the building without an adult encouraging me or some grandmother squeezing my cheeks while they told me they were praying for me. I can count more than ten people whom I'd consider my mentors before I was twenty-two years old! These were people outside of my family not letting me settle for anything but the potential they knew I had inside me. With that as my foundation, how could I not be resilient through hard times? Youth today need this more than ever.

Kids today have teachers who are overworked, exhausted from having to know how to work with all the special needs their students are facing. The "Coach Carters" are disappearing because of the systemic issues our education system is facing. Students don't look to teachers for guidance because they are skeptical and untrusting.

My son is one of those. He's been treated poorly and labelled by teachers, which has only caused him to question the motives of adults. He's defensive and guarded towards adults. I see this in so many youth people, especially the ones who need connection the most. Something has to be done to help our teachers out. Many of them enter education with the desire to make a difference in students' lives only to be covered in barriers preventing them from doing just that.

We've collectively lost consistent third spaces in which families can find community. While I was conducting one of my seminars with the Calgary Police staff, a social worker said to me, "I'm not a religious person, but one thing the church did when I was a kid was create a village. We need something like that again."

Regardless of what you believe about religion, we have yet to come up with something in communities that go beyond community centres, play places, or coffee shops. These are fantastic! In fact, as I write this chapter, I have my son and his friend playing at one of our local play places. The problem is, as I look around, I don't know anyone. If I were to show up at around the same time every week, with everyone else doing the same, then maybe there's the potential of meeting a few people. But even then, it's challenging, because as I look around for another glance, everyone is on their phones, and I'm on my laptop. What a social bunch we are.

I'm not okay with settling with things the way they are. We make sure we invite friends over after church every Sunday (when we can). My oldest son isn't a people person, but we ensure to bring into our home people who can be an example for him in his formative teen years. When it comes to developing friendships, I look for people who will love my sons as much as they love me. I want my friends to bring their children over for dinner so we can experience community as families, not just "ladies' nights out." We look for friends with whom we could go on holidays.

We also have some community-building ideas about creating global schooling opportunities for families to travel the world together. Stay tuned for that.

My oldest is still being homeschooled because I need him to make healthy connections with peers and adults who see his value and call it out. With my youngest still in school, I ensure his teacher and I are on the same page. I see the teacher as my son's village. I refuse to work against them. I want open communication so we can work together to see my youngest do the best he can.

I wonder what difference it would make it we became allies with our children's teachers. I wonder what it would be like if we could have constructive conversations that keep the child—not personal opinions—as the focus. If our kids knew our communication and partnership with their teachers (and other adults in their lives) were strong, I wonder what that could do for their trust of adults.

We've sunk so far into doing this parenting thing alone, we're creating the problem by talking down about other adults and isolating ourselves from one another. I don't think we even realize we're doing this. It's hard to get through life alone. After a while, we don't see what an effect it's had on us.

In today's world, more than ever, we have to take ownership of creating spaces of belonging for our children. We have to be intentional, or our kids will slip through the cracks. The great news is that it's possible. Begin to dream for your kids again. What can you cultivate for them in your home, at their school, on your street? Start to look into how you can creatively do this. Pull in some friends to do this with you.

Chapter Twelve
You Are Your Child's Prefrontal Cortex

HERE'S THE PART YOU'VE MOST LIKELY BEEN WAITING FOR: HOW DO YOU GET YOUR CHILD to calm down? How do you discipline?

Without everything we've discussed in previous chapters as your foundation, what we'll cover for the next few chapters in the book will become mere tools, tried again and failed. Connection must be something we cultivate in ourselves that we bring to our homes—then all you are about to read will work.

So how do you calm down a child raging? How do you ease an anxious child, or a teen struggling with depression? How do you reason with opposition?

I'll never forget one particular day when my son was just three years old. He was acting completely unmanageable. In a moment of desperation, I cried out, "Ben!… Dammit!" to which he replied, "Mom, my name is not 'Ben Dammit.'"

His cute comment broke my frustration and made me laugh, but it also brought to my awareness my own dysregulation. Sometimes while watching my son go berserk, I could see myself.

Our children learn how to reason from us. They learn regulation from us. They learn how to cope with large emotions by watching how *we* deal with *ours*. We often want our children to evaluate what they did wrong after a blow-up, or we want them to figure out what to do next time. The truth is, it's not going to do much unless we get a grip on our reactions first. If you want to calm your child down, learn to calm yourself down *first*. We need to make the switch from focusing on our children's behaviour to what's going on inside of us first so we can respond appropriately, in an emotionally steady state.

Earlier in the book, I mentioned the importance of being attuned, particularly with infants. Mirror neurons in the brain cause us to mirror others; their emotions speak to us and form us. As we grow, these mirror neurons continue to connect us to one another.

This is important to understand when trying to get your child to calm down. We need to understand a part of the brain from which all our reasoning and problem-solving stems—the prefrontal cortex, which doesn't fully develop until age twenty-five. That means we are all in this for the long haul. That means we'll need to repeat ourselves a gazillion times because they need us to. That means we need to be the voice of reason and problem-solving for our children—not only when they are two years old, but also when they are ten, sixteen, and twenty-one.

Storytelling helps little ones to process. We were having issues with our little one being explosive. He started telling me about his friend "Dave" (imaginary) who lost his temper. I thought this was a great opportunity to story-tell our way to a solution.

"How did Dave calm himself down?" I asked my son.

"His dad told him that everything was going to be okay," he replied.

Later in the day, when my son was melting down, I sat down next to him and said, "Everything is going to be okay." He calmed down. I'm glad I paid attention to his story, as it was able to give me a tool to help him later.

Being your child's voice of reason doesn't mean giving them advice or solutions when they are dysregulated or in meltdown mode. They won't be able to understand or even listen. When your child is flying off the handle, they're living in the back of their brain. All reasoning has been turned off, and there's no getting through to them until they are calm.

But you're probably asking, "That's the problem! How do I calm my child down?"

Let's get to that.

Connection creates room to learn reasoning. Our society is not set up for this to be easy. We're constantly on the move—going to work, taking our kids here and there to all kinds of activities while we get dinner through the drive-thru, etc. There's no time to connect face-to-face, yet that's the *one* thing they need.

If you want to change culture, sit down with your child and give them undivided attention for ten minutes a day. That alone could change the world in your home—or, at the very least, allow you to be more successful in helping them calm after a storm. When you put connection with your children as the priority, they see you as a safe refuge when they are facing storms of emotions. They will more likely calm down more quickly when they see you as safe. If they see you as someone who might lose it as well, it only sinks them further into their emotional state.

Self-regulation doesn't mean "behaving well." Regulation happens when the mind becomes integrated. We're able to escape our fight or flight and begin to reason. We can separate ourselves from others' emotions. Our environment influences the ability to regulate. When we suffer from dysregulation, it hinders our ability to connect. This then becomes a cycle in itself. Dysregulation in one person creates only more dysregulation in those around them. It's hard to break the cycle to become regulated in order to create connection.

Dysregulation hinders us from connecting socially with others. This is a problem because social interactions are exactly what we need to stay mentally healthy and away from addiction.

One of the greatest ways we can demonstrate connection to our children is to connect well with our partner. Parents who work together towards connection with one another teach their children connection. It's good for children to see healthy conflict resolution and leaning into tough conversations. It helps them form their conflict-resolution skills in their prefrontal cortex. We'll talk more about how marriage matters in the next few chapters.

Forming our children's ability to reason and problem-solve starts with this belief: "Everyone would do better if they could." Do you believe that—that everyone would do good if they could? How you connect is based on this belief.

For example, if I believe that my child is being rude, disruptive, and oppositional because they're rebellious, then I'll have a hard time connecting with them. I'll want to fix their behaviour and control them. When that doesn't work, military school starts looking mighty attractive.

However, when I see my child as doing the best they can with what they know, I can see myself as someone who can come alongside them to help them figure things out. You might wonder, "But what if I keep seeing the same behaviours and attitudes over and over?" Sometimes it takes repetition for new patterns of thinking and behaviour to sink in. Don't give up on them. Remember, their prefrontal cortex doesn't fully develop fully until age twenty-five. We're in this for the long haul.

The hardest thing I had to do when my son was dysregulated was making connection with him the priority over fixing his behaviour. The truth is, I just wanted to fix him. I wanted some tool, person, or program to fix his behaviour. I wanted the easy way out. But all that our kids want to know, especially when they're experiencing big emotions, is that they belong with us and that we'll hold them, despite how they behave. They need to know that we can handle their big emotions.

This doesn't mean we won't eventually work on behaviours, but connection must come first. They need to know they can trust us. There is no shortcut around this. Trust is built with consistency. It took me a year to build this, so hold on to your hat and get ready to ride for the long haul.

A little word on trust: When someone trusts you, your heart is open. When someone questions your trustworthiness, it creates walls of defence. Once that happens, we can't hear or process what's being said because we enter into emotional survival mode. If there's no trust, there's no connection. Building trust between you and your child is of utmost importance to building a mind that can regulate.

Going through crisis with our son took me from having "book smarts" to having to figure out, through trial and error, how connection has to be lived out. More error than trial, honestly. I'd never been more challenged in my life. I would read, "There is no fear in love," but there sure is a lot of uncertainty in learning to love. There's a lot of fear in taking the first step towards connection. Real love is when we and our children don't need to fear. We are loved; we are held. This is the real grit right here. We need to realize we're often not dealing with our children's behaviour but the ruptures in relationships that they're experiencing, starting with us.

Sometimes our children's behaviours push us over the edge of reason. Our goal in that moment is to manage our own emotions, rather than those of our children. If we fail to manage our own emotions, we could damage our relationship by saying things we don't mean, or shaming our child. The worst thing we can do is respond out of our own dysregulation, or send our children away, where anxiety only increases.

One of the most challenging things for me to learn has been to get a grip on controlling my big emotions so I can be the safe adult. I'm naturally a very emotional person. There are many times my boys, myself, and even my husband are all losing it at the same time. Where are the adults?

I create more problems when I allow my son's outbursts to affect me. My tears or my frustration only cause him to think he's alone to solve his own problems. He has no safe landing place when I can't hold his large emotions without losing it myself.

So how do you do that? How do you keep yourself (or pull yourself) together when your children are falling apart?

First, it's important to not take our children's outbursts personally. Far too often, I've told myself a story that's completely opposite from what's actually happening. One time, my son was losing it, and the story I thought to myself was that if I were a good mother, he wouldn't be freaking out. If he had a different mom, he wouldn't struggle.

We all know that this is far from the truth, but in heat of the moment, you can convince yourself of anything. I had to recognize that story and name it for what it was: shame. Once shame is exposed, it can be silenced, and we can gain perspective. When I think my son is behaving poorly because I'm not a good mother, the shame I feel will be projected onto him, since I'll do anything to remove that shame—mostly by trying to control his behaviour even more just to make myself feel better.

Work on your own regulation by ensuring you get your own time to yourself each day. You probably just laughed. *What time?* I was beyond frustrated that I was constantly being interrupted when I was trying to have alone time. How did I think I was ever going to get alone time in the middle of the day when my children were hungry? Or at night when they wouldn't go to bed?

For me, alone time happens between five and eight in the morning. It sucks, but it's only temporary. The truth is, one day, my kids won't be around, and I'll be able to have alone time all the time whenever I want (however, by then, my natural alarm clock will most likely wake me up every day five anyway). I am guaranteed quiet time in the early morning. As much as I didn't like it at first, I love it—and need it—now. Without pressing snooze, I get out of bed joyfully—albeit sluggishly—when my alarm clock goes off because being by myself is my favourite time of the day. I know that if I don't take this time for myself now, it's not going to happen.

Cultivate your creativity and your passions. Too many parents give up the things they love and that bring them joy when they become a parent. Granted, we can't exactly join a rock band and start touring North America, but we can dust off that old guitar and start to play again because it brings us joy.

For me, I've always loved to dance. I still teach dance once a week in the evenings, even after all these years. I don't know what I'd do without movement. It brings me so much joy, and it keeps me active and feeling young. I also love to read. I make sure to get times when I can read (or even write books, like this one). My husband and I just started making beautiful wood signs. He loves to tinker in the yard and plant flowers. We might not be able to pour into our passions the hours we used to, but that doesn't mean they have to be put up on the shelf altogether. The time you take to scroll through social media could instead be used to refresh your soul with things you love. Your mood, mental health, and yes, your family, will be better off for it. Don't accept the lie that you don't have the time. You do; we all do. We will always make time for whatever we truly value.

Clear your schedule. I mentioned this earlier (and more on this later in the book), but one of the reasons we can't handle outbursts is that we have no time for them. "Our little Jonny can't have a meltdown right now because he has to get to soccer practice!" The more we take out all the scheduled clutter in our lives, the more we can focus on what's *meaningful*. Not having meaning in our lives is often the undercurrent of our frustration.

Own yourself. I refer to self-care as "self-ownership" because that explains more of what I believe self-care means. We think self-care is a day away at a spa somewhere. When we don't get the spa, or the book, or the bubble bath without someone in our home losing it or needing us, we feel ripped off. We become frustrated and annoyed. It creates more tension in us than peace.

However, self-ownership is different. It means doing *whatever it takes* to take care of ourselves. That means doing the hard stuff. Eating properly, exercising, getting enough sleep—you know, the unsexy, un-Instagrammable stuff. Would I rather have a quiet bubble bath than lift my weights? You better believe it, but the weights mean I'm owning myself and my responsibility to be the safe adult my kids need.

Find delight in your child. Find the gold in them. There's plenty to criticize at times. Ignore it for a moment and look at your child. What makes you proud of them? What is it about them that you love? Choose to intentionally look for this once a day in your child and see the difference it makes in your mood towards them. My son's opposition is something I have learned to love. When I notice him questioning why things are the way they are, or not being easily influenced, I beam with pride for him and make sure to tell him that.

If we cultivate our own hearts, then we can be the safe adults for our children when they are in the middle of a storm. We don't hear this enough. It's not about reading books on how to calm your child; it's about calming ourselves and setting the example.

Chapter Thirteen
Behaviour Is Communication

FINALLY! THE SECTION ON DISCIPLINE! (AM I RIGHT?)

The thing about discipline is that doing it effectively will depend highly on your ability to look past your child's behaviour and see what's going on underneath.

When our children behave a certain way, they're communicating a *story*—a story they often don't know how to communicate with words, so it comes out in their actions. It requires us to dig. My oldest was treating his younger brother terribly. We were at our wits' end trying to stop this. I was finally able to sit down and ask my son what was really going on. At this point, he was able to share that he was feeling we were spending more time with his brother than with him. His behaviour was communicating his desire for attention. I'm glad I dug deeper rather than reacting to his behaviour because then we were able to adjust accordingly and work towards improving the situation.

Look at your children's behaviour and ask yourself, "Why are they yelling?" *Oh, maybe they don't know what to do with their big emotions right now.* "Why are they getting into trouble at school?" *Oh, maybe they're bored and need more challenge.* Kids tell us what they need to work on through misbehaviour. Your child's mistakes are a great opportunity for growth and learning.

Does your child feel understood? Connection is key for us to be able to feel understood. Remember this mantra: Connection before correction. This means you need to connect with your child before you correct them. You're likely going to want to correct first because it comes naturally to us, but if you connect with them and you'll uncover what's really going on. Underneath the behaviour is where the transformation is.

Your child's number-one concern is not their behaviour. They're mostly concerned with questions like, "Does Mom really like me?" "Am I good enough?" "Am I worthy of love?" etc. Proceed with care through interpreting what's going on the outside. Become curious about them. Ask them what's going on. They might be able to tell you; they might not. The times when they can't, you'll need to observe for a while and then move in with more specific questions to help you (and them) understand what's really happening. Be careful not to make it seem like an interrogation.

The trick is, you have to be consistent. It's not going to be easy. Keep showing up. Don't try this for two weeks and then just give up. This isn't a tool, remember? Parenting is a full-on relationship. Talk to me in a year when you've shown up and continued to show up in your child's life. They don't want your new "technique" to "fix" them; they want to know you are *for* them.

I'll never forget the time when my son said to me, "Mom, you're no hero." He keeps it real. He was reminding me that just because I showed up for a couple of days didn't mean anything to him. He wanted to know I would be safe for him for years, not days.

This is foundational for us to learn. We need to remember that shame takes hold of us when we reach out for connection and are rejected. Every time a child lashes out, they're reaching out for connection. If they're rejected or shut down, shame becomes the voice they hear, and shame takes a lot of years to undo. Kids who misbehave are often reacting to the shame they feel: "I'll reject you before you can reject me."

We need to be filling up our children's cups so that when we do need to correct, we are coming from a place of fullness. If it's been a while since you've filled up your child's cup with love and connection—which is determined by them, not you—that's your first step before you correct behaviour. Then, when you *do* need to correct, there's enough trust built for shame to be silenced and for them to engage fully in the growth they need.

The basics a child needs before correction are:

Do they feel you are a safe haven?

Can they make mistakes and not be shamed for them?

Do they feel you are a secure base who can handle their big emotions and not "lose it"?

Do they feel connected to you? (Or misunderstood by you?)

Is there trust between you and your child at the moment?

The most important thing we can do is change the environments that give way to our children misbehaving. This proactive approach takes the skill of knowing what's underneath their behaviour, such as when I discovered that the reason my oldest son was misbehaving at school (and being sent to the principal's office) was that he was boredom. Underneath his (mis)behaviour was boredom. So, I changed his environment (homeschooling).

"I can't homeschool my children," you might protest. But that's not the point; it's merely an example to help us realize that many times, our children's behaviour will change if we shift the environment that's creating it. Sometimes that will be possible; other times it won't be, and we'll need to walk our children through it.

When it comes to discipline, our usual "go-to" is to use threats. When that doesn't work, we up the ante with consequences and punishments. We can escalate very quickly from taking away the privilege of stripping them of all they have. Why do we do this? The typical pattern is that when our children act up, then we react, which causes them to react in an even bigger way (retaliation).

Our first step in discipline needs to look for what's under the behaviour. This doesn't mean are letting our children get away with everything. Boundaries matter. We will be covering that soon, so stay with me. Remember, our children need repetition in order to learn. They make the same mistakes a gazillion times before the light bulb goes off. Our discipline should be helping our children learn what they need to learn, not punishing them for getting it wrong. We need to keep our emotions steady when we discipline (teach) so we separate how their behaviour made us feel (upset, sad, angry) from what we what our children to learn.

Our children need to be clear about our expectations. It throws our kids off when they don't know what they are. If your child does something wrong regarding an expectation, you forgot to communicate, talk to your child. "I'm sorry that I didn't mention this was an expectation," then clarify your expectation.

Many children are afraid of messing up because they don't want to upset us. As a little girl, I would promise to myself daily that I wouldn't do anything "wrong" that day. I desperately wanted to please my parents. My son often says to me that disappointing me causes him much anxiety. We need to discipline in such a way as to develop a positive outlook and strengthen their prefrontal cortex (the place of reasoning and problem solving). When our kids are worried about upsetting us, they may be outwardly compliant, but they're still in the back of their brain, sometimes full of anxiety. This isn't what any of us parents want.

Before you respond to a mistake your child has made, ask yourself *why* they made the mistake. What do you want to teach them? What's the best way they can learn what you want to teach them? Is whatever you've done up until now working? Is it increasing connection, or causing disconnection? We all experience guilt or even shame when we feel our methods aren't working with our children.

Remember our mantra: This is a no-shame zone. Shame can suck it. The truth is, everyone does better when they know better. Most of us parents are trying the best we can with what we've been given. Our children show up with no manual. We didn't get a degree in parenting. We are left to try and figure it out. Show yourself compassion; from that place of self-compassion, be willing to learn and grow.

Our children become much more receptive to us when we seek to connect with them, not try to fix their outward behaviour. When we do the latter, they feel misunderstood because they're simply trying to communicate a deeper need. When that need isn't understood, they lose the ability to be receptive to correction. They become both frustrated and stressed because no one is helping them understand *why* they keep making the same mistakes. Behaviours will only increase if the underlying issue(s) aren't dealt with.

If our children don't feel understood by us, they won't receive correction. This tells us we need to connect with them more before we can correct behaviour and discipline. Trust me, this works. It sounds ridiculous, but I've tried the opposite and it only caused heartache and frustration for all parties involved. Changing my priority to connect first with my son has changed our relationship tremendously. He takes my correction like a champ (most days).

When we connect before we correct, it creates an atmosphere of calm and increases trust, which is crucial for the child and the parent-child relationship.

What about young kids and tantrums? Working with *any* child under five deserves a medal, in my opinion. You can't reason with them.

My grand explanations to my young sons would often only be met by blank stares and continued screams. It's important for us to remember that, just like a baby cries when they need something, little ones can't explain the deep emotions they're experiencing, so it comes out no different from a baby. We often assume they should just "be over it" by now.

But when little ones throw a fit, we need to find out what's *underneath* the behaviour in the same way we do with older children. Are they hungry? Tired?

Bored? Do they feel overwhelmed or overstimulated? I learned the times my son could (and couldn't) handle outings very quickly by noticing when and where his tantrums occurred. I learned what environments triggered him. We learn this only by listening and noticing what's happening when they experience a tantrum.

I can't tell you how many times I had to pick my son off the mall floor and carry him, kicking and screaming, to the car after a meltdown. I finally learned the times not to take him when he was tired, when the mall was crazy, or when he would be hungry. It seems simple, right? Yet it's hard to remember these things when you've been deprived of sleep for a couple of years.

It's important to see past the tantrum and figure out what our children need in the moment. We often scold our children for having a meltdown, but we need to remind ourselves that when they're acting out the most is when they need us the most. They're communicating; it's our job to figure it out. This means pausing. Don't react to your child right away. Don't feel the need to correct right away, either. Observe what's going on. Respond after you've observed and thought through what they need. Too often, we respond too quickly because the escalation in our children's emotions causes us to panic.

Don't give in. Breathe (deep breaths), take a moment to observe, then respond with what you feel they need. It could take a million guesses and tries, but eventually, we get it. Some say tantrums are attention-seeking. Of course they are! As a child, if you can't communicate with words and reasoning, you cry or scream (sometimes both) until someone pays attention.

Adults honestly aren't much different. How many husbands read the silent treatment or the slamming of cupboard doors as something more than just silence and slamming? Sure, it may take twenty years, but through the silence or slamming, wives are indeed telling a greater story that needs a master interpreter.

The point is, we never grow out of communicating through behaviour. Why would we expect anything different from our children, then?

There was a time I finally got this right. My husband and I were visiting family in St. Petersburg, Florida, and thought we would take our three-year-old son to Disney World for a day. I was so excited to show our son everything in the park!

Then it hit me. Maybe this was an unrealistic goal. Maybe we should go with our son's pace of what he could handle. So we did. It was a great morning, and he loved. Around one in the afternoon, I started hearing murmurs of cries from children my son's age all around. It began to get louder. I looked at my son. Because I was learning to observe his behaviour and what it was seeking to communicate, I could see he was almost at his tipping point to a full-on meltdown. We left the park just in time.

If only I could've *always* been that observant in my day-to-day interactions with him. How many meltdowns would I have avoided!

Whether your child is two years old communicating through tantrums, or thirteen (still communicating with tantrums), or an adult, remember, all behaviour is communication. Our job is to discover, "What are you trying to say?" Then, learn what's going on underneath and respond to *that*.

Under the behaviour is where the transformation happens.

Chapter Fourteen
Values-Based Discipline

MANY OF US DON'T HAVE A DISCIPLINE PHILOSOPHY. I DON'T THINK MANY OF US EVEN realized that's even an option.

To have a discipline philosophy, you need to be clear on your values. You need a clear understanding of what you actually want to accomplish when your child misbehaves. Do you know what your values are? What are the values you want to instil in your children by the time they leave your home at age nineteen, twenty-two, or even thirty?

My personal values are courage, compassion, and community. I wrote a whole book on my personal values, *Culture Rebel: Because the World Has Enough Desperate Housewives*, if you want to read more.

Many adults have forgotten about values, or have no clue what theirs are. When we know what our values are, we know what to fight for. Some people aren't brave with their lives because they don't know *why* they would be brave. Failure is faced with courage when we fail in attempting to live out our values. Failure sucks when it's just failure. When we feel like giving up, it's our values that keep us going.

Our values are our "why." That annoying question your child repeatedly asks—"But why?!"—can become a remarkable teachable moment with our children to communicate our values. Ask yourself: *Why* do you care about homework being completed? *Why* do you care about a curfew? *Why* do you care about manners? Figure out the value behind each one, and you're on track. Stop saying, "Because I said so." No values are communicated through that—only confusion and frustration.

When coming up with your values, you'll likely be tempted to have a list of twenty. Don't do that. Focus on two, maybe three. Your values should feel like you, not like mine or what you read in a book. They have to deeply resonate with you and reflect who you are at your best. They need to represent what you would be willing to live out, even when it's hard, because we have to do more than just know what our values are—we have to live them. Our children won't follow our values if they don't see us living them out. Living them out means what we say and what we do align. If they don't, we lose credibility with our children, and they reject the very values we stand for. Children can't stand hypocrisy. Intentions mean nothing to kids; rather, actions do.

What does your life look like when you're living out your values? Courage for me doesn't mean skydiving; courage looks like choosing to love when I want to run. My kids have seen me struggle with my value of courage. We're often afraid to have our kids see us struggle. I believe that if our kids see us living out our values when it's hard, it teaches them more about values, rather than us "preaching" at them about it.

How will you push through to live that value when it's difficult? Find a way to keep yourself accountable for living out your values. Find one person whom you trust to keep you accountable. Your family is also great feedback. If you want to keep it real, ask your child how you're doing—they'll tell you. They're generally pretty honest. Or ask your partner—they'll tell you, too.

What you spend your money on is a good indicator of your values. I call your credit card your "heart monitor" in my book, *Culture Rebel*. Our finances show us an honest picture of how we actually live, not how we intend to live. If you say you value health and you see McDonald's on your financial statement more times than you'd like, it's time to make some decisions to live what you value. If you say you value generosity but you've spent more money on yourself than anyone else in the past six months, then you've fooled yourself. This is the hard stuff to look at. It takes some serious guts to face yourself without shame.

How would you live differently if you truly lived from your values? We need to make brave changes to the sometimes-good things, not just bad, that are robbing us from truly living.

Many adults could use a boost of joy in their lives. Look around. Are adults joyful? Most aren't. They're stuck in jobs they hate, burdened with too much debt from buying into the idea that stuff equals happiness. There's so much more for us that could benefit our children. Our kids need to see that there's more to life than making money to pay for a house we can't afford and displaying our so-called perfect lives on Instagram. Take a long, hard look at what you'd like to value and see if your lifestyle and bank statement are measuring up. If not, change it. Everything that matters is hard. Do the hard stuff to make the changes you need to.

All parents know there's an art to picking your battles—especially the older your children get. How do you know what battle to pick if you don't know what values matter to you? My battle isn't stopping a fight between my boys; my battle is putting an end to the cruel words, because belonging is a huge value in my home. My battle isn't punishing my son for getting sent to the principal's office; my battle involves *why* he's getting sent to the principal's office—losing sight of his purpose and commitment. My battle is a callback to strong character, which is another one of my values.

Discipline isn't just about the temporary, but what you're building into your child for the future. I want my boys to be able to cultivate belonging in their own families in the future, and I want my son to be able to follow through with commitments, no matter how hard they are when he's an adult. I know the battles I choose to engage in are worth it, because I'm thinking ten to twenty years down the road. Of course, I'm human, so I mess up and get caught up in those silly battles that my values say I need to. I'm certainly not exempt!

I've never seen kids more devoid of values—integrity, character, showing up when you don't want to, honesty, loyalty—than I do today. I'm just not seeing it. Over the past twenty years that I've worked in schools, I've noticed values decline year after year, and right behind it, has come a decrease in family disconnection. For some reason, parenting has taken a decrease in transferring values. When I was growing up, my grandparents, who were boomers, were always instilling values—my Baby boomer parents too. I was never let off the hook to see a task through or follow up with my commitments.

What's happened?

Parents need to remember that discipline can serve a great purpose that goes beyond punishment or giving out what we think is a "natural consequence," which sometimes is just punishment in disguise. But when we have a discipline philosophy based on what our values are, instead of correcting behaviour, we correct what's going on that's distracting from the values we're trying to teach and instil. This, again, is getting to what's underneath the behaviour.

Remember, discipline means teaching. When your child doesn't get it right—and they often won't—these become teachable moments to pass on something far greater than a timeout. We can teach them to have to wait for what they want—emotional regulation, the art of following through with what we say we'll do, kindness, honour, integrity, belonging, etc.

We can pass on so many wonderful values to our children, but it won't be easy. We have to be willing to push through the tantrum, the yelling, the blame for us making their lives so miserable (that one's my favourite!). We also need to teach these things with empathy rather than smug sarcasm.

"Well, I guess that will teach you to be on time next time won't it?" is not an appropriate response.

Instead, we can respond with empathy: "That's rough you missed the opportunity to be in the school play. But I know next time, if you're on time, they'll let you audition."

It's best to think of yourself as a coach, guiding your child towards these values as a goal.

To teach our children values, we want to be able to help our children navigate their own and others' emotions so they know how to respond to various situations. For example, when my boys are arguing, I debrief with them afterwards. I ask my youngest how his brother's words made him feel (and vice versa).

Then, I ask what might have provoked the words. I do this because I want my boys to learn empathy towards each other. I want them to know how their words affect one another and to be aware of one another's feelings. I also want to teach my boys that repair is the most important thing we do in our home. When we have an argument, it's important to repair the relationship later. This goes beyond the unfelt, unmeaning "I'm sorry" they offer. These apologies come across sounding like, "Mom said I have to do this, so here's my 'sorry,' but I'm really not."

True empathy is so important in order to be able to identify with others' emotions.

When in a moment of discipline, it's important to speak firmly yet kindly. Our tone of voice can change everything. Our response creates a response. If we're angry or overly frustrated, it will affect whether our children can receive our correction. When your child is having a meltdown and losing it, this is not the time for any elaborative explanations. Say as little as possible, in one sentence if you can. Don't raise or lower your voice and don't add words. You'll need to repeat it.

For example, "Son, you need to go get your shoes on." That's all I need to repeat over and over. He will yell, react, flip out. But this isn't the time to

Unfortunately, seeking to motivate our children with rewards only reflects how anxious we are as parents, not on our children's ability to be motivated inwardly. I used to give my son a cookie from Starbucks every time he went to the dog park with me. It worked wonders! But guess what? I put myself in a trap because this meant he expected that cookie every time we went to the dog park. Now, years later, when I ask him to come with me to the dog park to take care of his dog, he doesn't want to come (because I stopped using the cookie reward). My "reward" plan backfired on me.

When we use rewards, we're making the task *our* idea instead of *theirs*. The best way to motivate your child is to have a strong connection as your foundation, and to use encouragement, not nagging (as my son calls it). What we don't realize when we motivate through rewards is that we can be communicating non-verbally that our children are valued only when they do what we want them to do. We don't want rewards to become our children's goal. This could lead to many problems in the future, such as being a sore loser, but the worst is if our children lose motivation or interest in something they loved. That's tragic.

Giving our children choices is one of the best ways we can motivate our children. Of course, the choices need to be age-appropriate. For example, when my son was in Grade Three and still in school, homework wasn't a "choice." Rather, *when* he did homework was a choice. At first, I thought doing homework right after school was a great idea. Why not get it out of the way? When I attempted to impose this idea onto my son—"Homework will be worked on when you get home from school"—there was immediate resistance and an outright rebellion.

We power-struggled for a week until I thought about giving him the choice of *when* he does homework. He decided he would watch a few of his favourite television shows and then do his homework. I was skeptical at first. If it were me in his shoes, the homework would never get done. However, this was my son, not me, and it worked brilliantly. The goal was to get the homework done, and because I gave him a choice, his motivation to get it done came from inside of him instead of being imposed by me.

Creating structure plays a large role in creating motivation in our children. Our children can't learn inner motivation if our lives are chaotic and devoid of structure. More on this later, but what I will say about it now is that the structure you provide for your home starts with you creating structure for yourself first, before creating structure for your children. If you want them to be more active, when are you scheduling that in for yourself? If you want them to take time to budget their money, are you modelling good budgeting? Again, it comes back to values. If you value health, you have to model it. If you value managing finances, you go first. You create structure in your home by first making time for the things you value first; everything else can wait. Anxiety rises in children when they don't have structure, and ADHD symptoms only increase.

I've also found from experience that natural consequences are the best teacher for my son. When he learns the hard way, which is incredibly hard for me to watch and not jump in and fix, he learns! For example, when my son entered Grade Seven and had a teacher who gave an unreasonable amount of homework, I let him choose whether he did it. (I don't recommend doing this with young children who need to learn work ethic for homework.)

If I would've forced my son to do his homework, he wouldn't have done it anyway. When I noticed that giving him a choice of when to do his homework wasn't working, I knew something was up. The amount of homework was legitimately overwhelming and unreasonable. Instead of going into Momma-will-fix-it mode, I said to him, "So what are you going to do?" He replied, "I'm not going to do my homework." I let him make this choice so he could learn from it.

I wish I could say that a couple of times of not doing his homework taught him a lesson. It didn't. My son's seventh-grade year was not good. His behaviour sunk, his attitude stunk, and he never did his homework. I let him play out his choice for a while, but then gave a choice when I saw his own decisions going too far. "Son, you are not being responsible. You are abusing the privilege of school. You can either do what school requires, or come home to be homeschooled."

There was his choice, and he chose to come home.

Some might find that to be flaky, but here's the thing: Once I stopped reacting and truly observed my son, I realized that after a full day of being at school, he could only handle about twenty minutes of homework, not hours. Knowing this, I realized that public school wasn't the best option for him. Homeschool allows him to do schoolwork during the day and have time to relax at night. His motivation for school is higher at home than it is within a school environment.

I'm only using this as an example. I'm not saying all children should be homeschooled. But think about what you can allow your child's decisions to teach them on their own or naturally play out in a way that's safe and doesn't harm them?

Having empathy is going to be key in helping your children be inwardly motivated, especially when we allow them to learn from natural consequences.

My friend's daughter once accidentally dropped her phone in a pool. The natural consequence was having to do the dishes for the next month in order to pay for the phone to be fixed. Empathy sounds like this: "Oh no—that's frustrating your phone fell in the pool. We'll get it fixed, and you'll do the dishes for a month to pay for it." On the flip side, shame sounds like this: "I've told you a million times not to take your phone to the pool! Now you'll have to do the dishes for a month to pay for it because you never listen!"

The key is to empathize with your child, no matter how stupid you think their decision was, or how much you don't like what they're feeling. When we don't empathize with our children, they shut down and become defensive. We get on their cases for their horrible attitude. Empathy breaks that cycle from starting.

But when we allow our values to navigate how we discipline and teach our children to become inwardly motivated, we see our children grow up to become resilient and strong. It's the harder road, but it's worth it.

Chapter Fifteen

Boundaries Matter

THE MAIN QUESTION I GET AFTER SPEAKING TO PARENTS ABOUT MY MESSAGE OF bringing our children closer is, "But what about boundaries? Do I just let them do whatever they want?"

No.

We bring our children closer with having boundaries. Children feel the most secure when there's clarity on boundaries and guidelines of what's acceptable and what's not. In order to do this, you need to be crystal clear on your values so that you know where you start and where you stop.

Just to recap something we've already covered, which is important to boundary setting, is that the only person you control is *you*. Becoming clear on your values so you know what boundaries you have is crucial to being able to communicate your boundaries and committing to them.

Because I value belonging, I won't tolerate being spoken to in a rude way. I commit to communicating that when I need to. The tone with which we communicate our boundaries is everything. I can say the same sentence in two different ways, and it will be heard in two different ways. It's important to communicate your boundaries in a firm yet kind way.

My values of connection and belonging help me create boundaries in my daily schedule. For example: I put my phone away after six o'clock in the evening so I can be present with my children. I don't pick up phone calls or answer texts when my children are around unless these were scheduled or there's an emergency. I made this decision because I value being able to be fully present for whomever I'm talking to. It's hard to fully engage when you're having to mime ninja moves to get your children to stop fighting while you're also trying to be present during a phone conversation.

My values also help me create my bedtime. I go to bed by ten o'clock at the latest because I value being able to connect peacefully with my children during the day. I get up at five every day in order to take care of myself in order to do so. If I didn't know my values, I would never have a strong enough "why" to commit to getting up that early!

What are some boundaries you need to put in place with your kids to take care of yourself? For example, "I will not tolerate being spoken to that way" or "I need my sleep in order to be a good parent; that's why it's bedtime."

What do you need to implement in order to ensure your children understand your boundaries? For example, "If you yell at me, I will walk away and talk to you when you're calm" or, "I will be going to bed at ten. Any conversations after that can wait until morning."

The clearer you are with your boundaries and the more you communicate them with your family, the more secure both you and your children will feel. This feeds positive connection and avoids anyone feeling as though they're walking on eggshells, which only exacerbates anxiety and disconnection.

We know we're supposed to have boundaries. The problem is that many have no idea what boundaries are and how to implement them. Here's what most people don't know about boundaries: They teach others how to treat you, but, more importantly, how you should be treated. How do you know how you want to be treated? Often, we're not angry with people when we've felt that we've been walked over; we're angry at ourselves for letting them do it. You teach people how to treat you by your boundaries or lack thereof. It's a dangerous pattern for us to believe that we deserve toxic relationships or to be treated poorly. We need to know our value in order to have healthy boundaries.

Here are some tips for creating boundaries grounded in value so you and your relationships thrive:

The first boundary you need to have in place is to look to control yourself only. I control no one but me. We get into so much trouble when we try to control others. People without boundaries are notorious for this, because they've bought into the belief that others determine their own happiness or success. The truth is, you don't control your children, your partner, your employees, your co-workers, your friends—just you. Just you. That's it. As soon as you seek to control anyone else, you are dependant. The irony is the control you seek just left you completely out of control and at everyone's mercy.

The second boundary is to discover why others' moods and behaviours affect yours and reconcile it so you can live peacefully without having others' emotions directly affecting yours. The moods of others—even if they live in close proximity to you—honestly don't have to affect you. You don't have to go through life reacting to everyone else around you. To reconcile this, you need to do some digging into why other people's moods affect yours.

For me, I realized I had lived most of my life responding to the moods of others because I was always seeking approval. Once I started reminding myself that I didn't need the approval of others, their moods, attitudes, and actions also stopped affecting mine. I took everything far less personally. What a gift to myself—and to them!

The third boundary is to get clear on what you want to say "yes" to so you know when to say "no." Your life and the lives of others will benefit tremendously. Saying "no" is kind.

"I have such a hard time saying no."

I hear this all the time. What we don't realize is how cruel this is to ourselves and others. We end up doing things we resent, and it drains the life out of us, sometimes leading to burnout. This often leads us to a cycle of blame on others for "making" us do things we never wanted to do in the first place. The truth is, no one can make you do anything. You're a grown adult with the power to make decisions! If you choose to say "yes" to something, then it's all on you. Own your decisions. Get clear on what you want to say "no" to. The more "no's" you say, the more you can say "yes" to things that truly bring you to life! This makes you a more pleasant person to be around, and fills your life with joy. You feel alive and vibrant.

It's possible to say "no" with kindness. "Thank you for this offer, but it's not for me." "It sounds amazing, but no thanks." "Love what you're doing. My capacity is full, but you have my support."

The fourth boundary is to set people free from your expectations. It's here you'll find your freedom. No one owes you anything. Let me repeat that: No one owes you anything. Your children owe you nothing. Your partner owes you nothing. Your friends owe you nothing. Your boss owes you nothing. Your employees owe you nothing. The sooner this sinks in, the more fulfilling your relationships will be.

Every time I experience what I consider a "rotten" Mother's Day, it's because I've expected too much from my children. Birthdays have bombed when I had unrealistic hopes from my friends. My marriage has suffered when I expected my husband to completely fulfill me. My marriage took a 180-degree turn when I stopped relying on my husband to make me happy. My relationship with my children is so much better when I stop reminding them of everything I do for them and how much they "should" appreciate me. My friendships are fulfilling when I enjoy meaningful moments with others, with no strings attached. My work relationships are enjoyable when I focus on my own responsibilities and not on how much I'm doing compared to everyone else.

Is it possible to still believe the best about people, be generous and forgiving, *and* have boundaries? The belief that "everyone is doing the best they can" is called, "The assumption of positive intent." In order to believe this, we must have boundaries. The people who are the most generous, the most forgiving, and are the most gracious towards others are people with clear boundaries. Boundaries will take intention. Instead of attempting to implement them all at once, why not take a week or two to focus on one. Seeing these become natural will greatly improve your quality of life and relationships.

Just the other week, I was able to take dance class, something I don't get to do very often. At the end of the class, I got a text from my husband: "You forgot to feed the kids before you left. I had to stop what I was doing to feed them. Could you please make sure they eat before you leave next time?"

It was a fair request; however, it triggered me. Back when we were in crisis mode, I used to receive frustrated texts from my husband while I was out, with him telling me things that were going on at home that I couldn't control. I was usually at work when these texts would come in. They left me feeling helpless. I caught myself viewing this present-day text through the same lens as past texts. I had to take a moment to pause and remind myself of the story I was telling myself. I was upset because I *always* offer to feed my kids, but that particular evening, they didn't want to eat because they weren't hungry. Was he saying he thought I was incompetent as a mother? I had to put my own story aside and choose to see what my husband was saying through his eyes. Once I did that, I could see his frustration.

I came home and was honest about how the text had triggered me. I then set up a boundary that would help me. I asked that we talk face-to-face about issues when I come home rather than through texts when I'm away and can do nothing about the situation. I also created a boundary for my children that if they are offered food before I leave and refuse, then they are responsible for their own dinner. Simple.

What could have been a huge argument and playing the blame game was simply solved by pausing to unveil the story I was telling myself, choosing empathy for seeing the situation through my partner's eyes, and creating boundaries that would solve the problem for next time while respectfully advocating for myself. It really can be that easy.

It's important to teach our children to have boundaries as well. The issue of bullying is at an all-time high. We need to teach our children how to have healthy boundaries towards others who hurt them at school. What if we taught them to, instead of reacting, say, "I don't like how you're treating me" or to use powerful statements that create healthy boundaries, like, "I don't deserve to be treated this way." We can also teach our children to call the bully up by saying to them, "You can do better than this."

We can teach our children to have boundaries rather than reactions, respect instead of retaliation. It's possible to have braver conversations like this, but in order to teach our kids to do this, they need to see us model this. If our kids hear us talking about some "idiot" at work and don't hear us dealing with them in the same way we ask our kids to deal with difficult kids at school, they'll model the pattern we *live*, not what we *say*.

I'm teaching my son how to express his feelings to others respectfully, how to be self-aware, and how to be able to communicate his needs and emotions. It's tough for him; in fact, it's tough for most people. Many of us would rather avoid conflict at any cost. This doesn't help anyone. We need to be willing to be the first to say, "I'm sorry," to be the one who steps up to the plate to engage in hard conversations so we can teach our kids how to do the same. How can we teach our kids to advocate respectfully for themselves when we're burying our heads in the sand when a relational conflict arises in our personal lives or at work.

You can't bring anyone closer without having clear boundaries you've set for yourself. A lack of boundaries will always disconnect people. You need to define where you start and where you end. As different situations crop up, you'll find out where your boundaries need to be. Create them, communicate them, and watch your family become better connected.

Chapter Sixteen
Redesign Your Home

"WHAT ARE YOU NOTICING ABOUT MENTAL HEALTH FROM YOUR CONTEXT?" WAS A question I asked all registrants for an annual conference I host on Bell Let's Talk Day.

The answers were eye-opening. From business leaders, to teachers, to teens, to mental health care workers, the common theme that came up was a lack of support.

"I am struggling to figure an answer to this question," one teacher responded. "As a mom and educator, I see too many young people dying because of lack of supports and lack of understanding. I spent yesterday in the ER with yet another student who attempted suicide. Two funerals in eight months and so, so, so many visits to the hospital for my daughter, her best friend, my friend's daughter."

I personally experienced a large gap in our mental health care system when we were in crisis with our son. We had been trying to get help for him, only to find ourselves referred here and there. We hit so many dead ends. The amount of anxiety our son went through to actually go to these appointments, and then only to see it was for nothing, was incredibly disheartening. It seemed our only option to get the help he needed was to pay a pretty penny.

Yet who can afford this?

When you're a parent in crisis, you don't know where to look. Too many appointments are exhausting. And what about work? I can't tell you how much work I missed. Many parents can't afford to miss work. This has opened my eyes to realize there are kids from good families who end up in group homes or correctional facilities. It takes too long to get them the help they need, or they fall through the cracks.

I see these kids and families in crisis all the time. It's such an injustice. The medical system is taxed, and parents are exhausted just trying to find the proper help. There's got to be a better way to solve this.

When it comes to getting your child professional help, you have to do it when they are experiencing the small window when they are open to it. This makes the task all the more complicated if you're on a two-year waiting list. I've seen disgruntled teens in the waiting room.

At one point, my son told me, "I'll tell that counsellor anything she wants to hear, just to get out of there." I found I eventually stopped bringing my son to his counselling appointments. I would show up and found it much more effective to talk with the counsellor on my own about the various issues we were facing at home. I received counselling and then applied what I learned in our home. If your child isn't open to counselling, this could be a great option for you.

Going through mental health concerns with your child is difficult, no matter what degree. What does it look like when all the books have been read, techniques applied, and the fight only continues? You hold on, and then you hold on some more. You stay in the mess when you feel like throwing in the towel. You bring them closer, even through the pain, their refusal to accept your love, and your weakness to give into anger. When you're in the middle of all this, words don't come easy (or even at all). Maybe that's all okay. Maybe words don't have to express. Maybe fewer words keep it sacred.

I can't even count how many questionnaires I filled out and interview questions I had regarding my children and my parenting being in the mental health system. Each question screamed at my inadequacy. It was painful to speak the answers that led our family to crisis. The hardest questionnaire to fill out was ACES, which is a way for psychologists to determine trauma and whether your child might deal with a mental health crisis in the future and even critical illness. A score of four or higher means "at risk." Both my boys scored four. I can't even begin to describe the shame and desperation I felt in that moment.

I recall the amount of time I spent in the hospital waiting room that summer. I missed being in nature, biking, walking, just enjoying the outdoors in general. There were so many monotonous, lifeless, passionless days going through the mundane routine of hospital visits to counselling sessions.

In those weeks in the hospital, I had to make room for creative things that would fill my soul. I felt guilty for doing this, but in the end, it was refreshing. It's the best advice I can give anyone going through a crisis with a child being hospitalized. Make sure you take time for a walk or something that fills you, even if only for a moment. You'll be more present, more engaged, and more hopeful than if you didn't.

My favourite time of day was at dusk when the sky was painted gold by the setting sun. I needed to sit under its warmth. It was there each day that my soul found rest, even though my physical rest was non-existent. I heard God whisper to me, "Who told you to fear? Courage is yours. Take it."

We often want quick-fix cures only. We give doctors, counsellors, even God timelines that only add to our anxiety and questions when they don't meet our expectations. The truth is that the journey is unknown. It's better to surrender to the unknown. The character being created in us during hard times is a jewel. It not only assists our journey, but also allows for empathy and compassion for others to grow as well. Through pain, we discover the opportunity to make a difference if our eyes are open and our hands are ready.

Coming home from the hospital was the start of a long journey of healing. The Christmas holiday after our crisis was hard. I found myself weeping on numerous occasions. I had been learning about the power of negative emotions being a clue to something deeper going on inside that isn't meant to be ignored. We so often push down feelings of anger and sadness to appeal to the happy emotions we want to achieve or believe we should have. Yet not to listen to sadness or anger is to ignore something that's hindering health and wholeness. That season, I learned to let go of what I thought I should feel and allowed my soul to be naked. I let myself feel sadness and gave it permission to search me on the inside. It was uncomfortable and strange, but I let go of happiness as a goal and welcomed God to pour healing into my weariness. It was the beginning of my own healing so that I could bring healing to my family.

I remember the day I finally laughed from the gut during the dark season our family had faced. A friend reminded me that experiencing joy even in the midst of life's turmoil is not only a choice offered to us but can also be a reality—if we embrace it. Laughter reminds me that everything is going to be okay. That's something no tough experience can steal. Hope is always an option. Laughter heals.

So what do you do in the hardest times of your life? You stand there. Don't let anything move you. When the wind of doubt threatens to throw you off your place, you plant your feet firmer. When obstacles hurl themselves towards you, don't back down. When you are about to be pushed over by the weight of hardship, lean in and push against it. It's harder to stand than to move. It's hard to stand still and face your doubt square in the face, to be honest with your inner emotions, to have the courage to believe. It goes against the very fabric of our culture to stand and still believe, when the message everywhere is to be always and run to things that will help make it all better—shopping, another coffee, volunteering, a promotion, a night on the town, a new shade of lipstick—but all it does is keep us in its grip, only to repeat the cycle again, leaving us empty.

There is *hope*. We have to stop treating mental illness like it's some incurable disease. There are things we can do to see these issues significantly lessen and see our children free to live life without the prison of anxiety or depression. This is what drives me to continue to fight for the mental freedom of our children and families.

The rest of this chapter is about what I did to pick up the pieces of our brokenness and to completely redesign our home. I don't mean redecorating; I mean the total upheaval of our emotional environment, starting with inside of me.

As you read about how I redesigned my home, I would like you to remember that this took four years of taking baby steps. There were days when I could barely make it out of bed. I celebrated small wins, like eating breakfast or taking a shower. Coming out of crisis takes more time to recover than we think. Regular life is exhausting enough already. These changes are important, but they're only sustainable if you take them step by step, focusing on them one at a time.

I suggest focusing on one per month. At the end of the month, if you need more time, take it. You want lasting change. Change that lasts is slow-cooked. Take your time and be honest with your family about your journey.

Are you ready to create change? Focusing on creating structure in these three areas can redesign the most important aspect of your home: you. We create environments by what we bring to them. These areas can do a complete makeover of your entire life and your children's lives. It will take an incredible amount of courage to look at them, and even more bravery to implement them, but if you do, the life you and your family desire is there for the taking. Anxiety and depression lessen in environments that have a grip on the following areas.

The first thing you need to do is redesign your **schedule**. Do you find yourself rushed and busy with very little margin? Our schedules are what either create room for peace or chaos in our inner lives, which, in turn, affect the environments we create.

Redesigning your schedule can completely transform your home. Look closely at your wake-up time. Do you give yourself enough time in the morning to wake up without rushing? Getting in a workout or some movement every day is important. What time of the day works best? Morning? If so, wake up so you have time for that. Don't just jump out of bed and start your day hustling. A morning routine of deep breathing, prayer, and coffee (or tea) can do wonders for your levels of peace for the rest of the day.

Do you have time scheduled to eat? Make sure to schedule in times to eat properly so you're not just rushing through your food while you work on the run. Some families have their schedules packed tightly with sports, lessons, and activities that they never have any downtime during the evenings or weekends.

It's important to look at our schedules and clear it as much as possible so we have downtime to recoup. So let's take our crazy, busy calendars and rip them up. No, this doesn't mean we do nothing; but we can get so busy putting our kids in all sorts of programs to keep them occupied only to find we haven't spent any meaningful time with them at all.

Are you getting enough sleep? Do you have a routine that allows yourself to unwind after the day, or do you crash into bed exhausted from the day? Having a routine to relax before bed, no matter what your bedtime, is important, and can do wonders for your health and home.

Redesigning our schedule means saying "no" to certain things so that we can say "yes" to making life simple. I learned that with my son's issues, every day, or sometimes even every minute, can have a switch in challenges. If life isn't simple enough, it becomes exhausting to have the energy to face those challenges. Sometimes we have to fight for our children. Our sacrifices matter and it's a short season compared to the rest of our lives. Peace is in the perimeter we create for our kids.

This is what each day looks like for me (remember, this is an example):

five in the morning: wake up, coffee, pray, read, plan the day
six: write
seven: daily workout in our makeshift home gym
seven-thirty: kids up and fed
eight-thirty: leave for school to drop off my youngest
nine: dog park walk
nine-thirty to three (in the afternoon): work and homeschooling
three-fifteen: school pick-up

No more work for the day. The evening is for family. No exceptions. I'm available.

eight: get ready for bed and our family's guilty pleasure of "Survivor" on Apple TV.

ten: bedtime

Every. Single. Day. The only exception is when I travel or have a speaking gig, for which my limit is once a month for travel and only out two nights a week.

Giving my life a structure tells me when to say "yes" and when to say "no" to things. It gives my children predictability in the midst of my entrepreneurship, making them feel secure. It gives me a peaceful heart because I'm grounded. Curveballs don't throw me off; interruptions don't irritate me.

This is one practical way I've learned what it looks like to bring the hurting closer—providing structure, which is actually self-care so that I can care for my family.

I fight for simplicity, but I'm discovering there are times in our lives that just aren't simple. I'm learning to surrender. Listen to your season. Don't feel guilty for the things you need to drop to readjust. Every season will require something different out of you and bring a new gift to you.

The second thing you need to do is redesign your finances. I got tired of hearing my husband say, "We have no money!" so I took over our personal finances. I wrote down every little thing we spent each week and weekly compared it to our budget. I summarized all that came in as income and what went out each month and realized: "Wow, we have no money!" Turns out the husband was right. (Don't tell him that.)

Being the visionary I am, I started to use our monthly finances to project what was possible. I was able to project how many contracts I would need per month to meet our budget, rather than just "hoping" everything would turn out. When you're an entrepreneur without a fixed income, this is an absolute must. I remember doing a yearend report of how we did financially. I was able to see exactly how much came in and how much we spent on food, gas, shopping, and even Starbucks. I was able to notice where we could tighten and improve so we could put more of our money towards our values (which isn't Starbucks).

I could see which months that work was busier than others, so I can now forecast my year and pinpoint when I need to get out there and share the amazing work that we do with helping youth in schools and families. I was able to create a new budget centred on our values and goals.

It's a powerful feeling to not have to guess, but to actually have a financial plan in place that gives vision for the future. Our new budget is going to make more room to give to others, travel, and spend time as a family.

One of the best things we ever did as a family was to sit down and make a list of our values. This now determines what we spend our money on, including Christmas. One of our values is travel, so we spend less on presents so we can travel. Each of our children receives one present, and they are okay with that, because they're part of the conversation around our values. This has helped navigate conversations around allowance and needless spending. They understand more now when the answer is "no" because they understand *why*—they helped design our values.

I hear so many say, "I want to make more money so I can give back and be generous!"

Giving back and being generous starts when you have little. Generosity flows out of an abundant mindset that has little to do with how much income you make. Start now. You may not be able to give $1,000, but you can give a dollar. Generosity is a mindset. The best way to be able to be generous is to commit yourself to stewarding your finances well.

The stress that most individuals or couples experience is over finances. Do you know what your monthly expenses are? Do you know how much money comes in every month? Do you keep to spending only what you have, or are you racking up credit card debt or your line of credit? Here's how to take control of your finances:

1. Find out what all your monthly expenses are and write them down or document them into a computer program of choice.
2. Find out exactly what you bring in financially per month.
3. Create a budget based on only spending what comes in. I highly recommend creating a budget based on your values. If you value travel, make sure you include a savings fund for travel, no matter how small it may be for now. If you value education, saving, eating out with friends— those should be reflected in your budget.
4. Write down everything you buy. I document everything we buy on my phone in the "Notes" app. Place items into categories: groceries, vehicle, house, etc., and tally the items up every week and month and compare it to your budget to see if you are on track. If you've strayed off path,

you will be able to quickly notice that and make a plan to get back on course.

The third thing you need to do is redesign your **work**. Research is showing that people disconnected from meaningful work are becoming more depressed. We have to take a hard look at whether our work is causing us unneeded stress. Is your workplace adding meaning to your life or draining it?

However, that being said, even jobs devoid of personal meaning can be purposeful to fund our dreams. For example, if you are an artist but can't survive on painting alone, the part-time job at the restaurant might give you flexibility and funds to do what fulfills you. The point is to look at your work and see if it is adding value to your life and if it aligns with your values. If not, you might need to take a brave step and create an exit strategy in order to do what fulfills you and allows you to have the life with your family you desire. You might be able to do that now or create a five-year exit strategy plan. Creating a plan relieves you from feeling trapped, and also gives you permission to dream again.

Redesigning these three aspects of your life's structure (schedule, finances, work) can completely transform your inner life, which will spill over to your family. You are the adult and CEO of your home. No one is going to create intention around these items but *you*. The environment you create comes down to how intentional you are about creating health in all three areas.

The final thing we need to do as parents is to take care of ourselves. Stop "liking" self-care posts on Instagram and start taking care of yourself. It doesn't matter if you have a child with mental health issues or not. We parents owe it to our families to make sure we're taking good care of ourselves. Denying myself of my self-care items (morning quiet time, workouts, eating healthfully, getting enough sleep) means everyone suffers. I need to make the sacrifice of getting up a bit earlier. I need to prepare my food on the weekends.

Other ways I can help prevent potential stress is getting my kids ready a bit earlier so we're not rushed out the door, creating a structure at home that's predictable and helps my children and I have downtime, time for creativity, and time for proper sleep. It's not rocket science, but being committed to this can do wonders for mental health. Take care of yourself first, but remember, that means something comes second.

Many use self-care as a reason to not serve those whom we love. That's why I call it self-ownership instead. I'm the CEO of this body and this house I lead with my husband. I take care of myself by doing the all hard stuff we just covered in this chapter so I can take care of those I love.

When it comes to self-ownership, remember that no one is going to do it for you. In order for me to be present for my kids and family, I make sure I get time alone each day in the mornings, as I've mentioned. My current goal is to work at eating well and drinking plenty of water.

When it comes to self-ownership and redesigning your life and home, stop shaming yourself for all the things you aren't doing or can't do on this list. Don't sweat the technique. Make for yourself monthly goals and tackle one thing at a time. For example, I didn't get a grip on our schedule, finances, and work all at once. I took each one, bit by bit. I mastered one at a time to form a new habit, and then moved on to the next one. Give yourself permission to take it day by day and celebrate your wins. Self-ownership is the hard stuff, but it's the hard stuff worth doing. It will make an incredible difference in redesigning your home and rewriting your story.

Chapter Seventeen
Your Marriage Matters

"WHY DID YOU MAKE DADDY CRY?"—MY SON, AT AGE SIX

This is a whole other book, but too important to not mention in this one. Your marriage matters deeply in the life of your family. Your commitment to your partner, the relationships you bring into the home, is the number-one ingredient of creating either an emotionally safe environment or not.

This year, my husband and I will be married twenty years, and we have just been getting along in the last year. I say this as a joke, but in many ways, it's true. My husband and I have struggled to see eye-to-eye for almost our entire marriage. We are both extremely stubborn and have not been willing to bend in many areas. The reason we've finally been able to get along is that I learned I can't control him. He also stopped trying to control me as well.

Over the last few years, I've learned to lay down my rights and my agenda for him. This has not meant losing who I am, or him losing who he is; rather, it has looked like laying down our agendas to be able to see one another.

In our children's younger years, I didn't realize how much our marital strife was affecting them. It was causing them to live in the back of the brain. They felt anxious, not sure of when Mommy and Daddy were going to fight again. When our relationship suffers, our children suffer, but when our relationship flourishes, so do our children.

Relationships is a hard topic for many because it often carries with it scars and brokenness. There are many who are single parenting, or those who don't feel their partner supports them. Conflict in the home causes distress in our children and can have long-lasting effects, including ADHD, depression, anxiety, and oppositional defiance.

Love is such a risk. What if we risked our love for a lifetime, only to find it was never returned? We can sacrifice everything for someone close to us and they might still end up leaving or greatly disappointing us, even going as far as betrayal or downright cruelty. We can never get that time back.

When it comes to love, there's no guarantee. But here's the truth: People might turn on you, humiliate you, even devastate you, but that's not what's important. What matters most is not whether *others* change, but whether *we* change. People can't change this fact: If we love well, we will live well. No one can steal what's inside of us without our permission. Therefore I will not hate my partner; I will choose to love them when I am not loved back. I will choose love when I'm hurt and disappointed, betrayed, and rejected. I will choose to love with no expectations, no conditions, no demands, and in this life, I will find life when I learn to lay mine down.

Love is patient with others when you feel they deserve less.

Love is kind when you are right, but you choose kindness anyway.

Love does not envy when others succeed.

Love does not boast when feelings of entitlement, enlightenment and arrival superimpose.

It is not proud. It realizes you've come a long way, baby, but it's still a ways to go.

It is not self-seeking, but looks to the needs of others.

It is not easily angered. It acknowledges feelings, but practices a lot of empathy.

It keeps no records of wrongs.

(No records. Read that again.)

It does not delight when bad things happen to someone they don't like.

Love is happy when truth prevails, yet it always protects and covers others, knowing that no one wakes up in the morning wanting to be a jerk. It always chooses to trust and hope.

It keeps going no matter what.[3]

---

[3] Paraphrased from 1 Corinthians 13 (NIV)

Marriage has taught me that if all I gain at the end of my life is love—not achievements, wealth, success, dreams, but to be able to truly love—then I've lived well. I've learned the more you judge, the less you love. Whom do I judge most? My husband. Keeping love and connection strong is more important than holding on to being right.

What does this look like in the real world?

There was one day I did the laundry, the dishes, the vacuuming, filled 300 envelopes for a mailout, took the dogs for a walk, and took out the garbage, all while having a headache and taking care of my oldest son, who was sick, and our youngest, who had boundless energy and seemed intent on destroying the home. It had been one of the roughest "Mom-at-home" days I'd ever experienced.

My husband came home from work, and without even seeing the chaos happening around him in our home, and the exhaustion on my face, he blurted out, "I had the worst day today."

In my deep frustration and even anger, I blurted back, "Nobody cares!!"

"Nobody cares."

There's some real-life married-with-children language.

I had some serious armour on that day. Armour saying, "Don't touch me. You don't know me. You don't understand me."

What would it have looked like if I had taken off my armour in that moment, and allowed myself to show up, being fully seen by my husband? It might have sounded more like, "Honey, I know you had a rough day, but look around. I'm drowning here. I need you to see me right now so I can be able to see you."

Armour itself isn't wrong. Sometimes armour is wise. It's a way of protecting from those who haven't learned how to hold us in our vulnerability. Good armour looks like healthy boundaries, knowing where you start and finish, and being firm but kind in the communication of those boundaries. It also means making a list of people whom you trust, whose opinions really matter to you, so when someone shares an opinion that hurts, you dust the words off if they're not on your "list."

Lastly, healthy armour means learning to communicate with courageous statements like, "I want to feel heard, I want to be seen as I truly am, I want to work out our differences," rather than armoured statements like, "I don't need you!" or "I'll show you" or "I don't care what you think!" When we feel we're being attacked by our partner (and others), we put up our defences or up the ante: "Well, did you know that you… (fill in the blank)?"

We forget to bring one another closer by laying down our self to listen to the other person. Defensive statements like, "I'm not listening to her because she's just being ridiculous!" or "He never helps out!" will cause only further separation and even confirm what the other believes about their partner (or about themselves).

"I knew he only cared about himself. I'm alone in this world."

"I knew she was crazy. Must be her time of month or she's going through some weird hormonal thing."

"He doesn't appreciate me."

"She's mean."

"He doesn't care."

"He…"

"She…"

Courageous marriages look like this:

When it's hard, stay
> When it's painful, stay
> When it's boring, stay
> When it's unfair, stay
> When it's lonely, stay. (Christine Caine)

I can't write a chapter on marriage without including the elephant in the room—adultery. It's that subject no one opens up about, despite the rising amount of married couples who have confessed to either having an affair or cheating on their partner emotionally. In today's society, it's socially acceptable to have a "look but don't touch" mentality when it comes to our marriages.

We have no problems "checking out" other people, as long as we're not sleeping with them. Yet even getting into the sack with someone other than our spouse has become glorified by some top shows that are on TV today and through songs on the radio. It's considered normal.

It could start with dissatisfaction with our marriage. The tall, dark, handsome man we married is maybe now the bulging, bald, tired man we see before us. It could start with a distance that can so easily be created in marriage by work, newborns, kids, and general busyness. It could start with feeling forgotten and ordinary—wanting someone to make us feel sexy again. It could start with a flirty smile in the hall at work. It could start with spending too much time with that one person.

My husband and I are pretty open with each other. I told him it's not the tall, dark, handsome, fit man who would be my downfall; it would be the man who's really nice to me. If that was timed perfectly during a season when my hubby hadn't had a lot of time to pay attention to me, then there'd be big trouble. Unfortunately, this happened to me. I didn't commit adultery, but I experienced a time when I was put in a compromising situation that could have greatly damaged our marriage.

I realized, in those moments, that adultery and disconnection from a spouse are easier than we think. The most humbling thing I ever did was honesty with my husband about the whole experience. However, that moment was also the beginning of a turning point for our marriage.

It's so important to keep leaning into one another, even during seasons of disconnection, miscommunication, or misunderstandings. We don't realize it at the moment, but offence blinds us. We are either walking towards connection with our partner or away from it. I've had so many women tell me about the pain they experienced after adulterous relationships, realizing how blind they were and the despair they felt from greatly damaging, or ending, their marital relationship. If you're in that place right now, remember, it's going to be painful either way—to face yourself after cheating, or to work out all the challenges in your marriage. Pick your pain. I pray you to pick the latter. My husband and I just celebrated our twenty-year wedding anniversary. We've made it through many heartaches and found a greater love than we've ever known.

How would you rate the relationship you have with your partner at this moment? Is there anything hindering the relationship? (If you are currently in an unsafe/abusive relationship, you need to take action to remove yourself and your children from it.)

Is there any part of the relationship that has become strained because of not making sense of your own stories? Is there a chance to talk openly about these things? What do you dream of for your relationship? What would it take to see that become a reality? What needs to change on your end?

Chapter Eighteen
Resilience Is in the Repair

THIS VERY WELL COULD BE MY FAVOURITE CHAPTER, BECAUSE IF, WHILE READING THIS book, there have been any moments up to now when you've thought, "Well, that's just great. I've messed my kid up *completely*. I might as well just throw in the towel!" then this chapter is about the hope that rises, despite our imperfection.

If you don't remember anything you've read, remember this chapter, because it's the secret sauce. It's not about parenting perfectly that will make the difference for your child; rather, it's about how you repair the relationship after a rupture or a blowout.

I had one of the toughest days with my son I had in years. As I've mentioned with my oldest son, depression rears its ugly head as anger and aggression. This one particular day, he went off the deep end, and in the midst of his meltdown, he said some things that truly triggered me. I fell into it hook, line, and sinker, and completely lost it.

Mayday, mayday! Down I went spiralling into my own reaction. Where was the adult who could handle his big emotions? Apparently, she had left the building. Of course, this only made everything worse. Shame was screaming in my ear that day. What kind of parent did I think I was? I had failed. I felt horrible.

But then I remembered that what counts is how we *repair* after a rupture that matters. I dried my eyes, went to my son, and we cried and apologized and forgave one another. This is what matters. This is what determines whether or not your family makes it. This is what teaches your child connection. No one can be peaceful and perfect all the time. Your family will have ruptures, and yes—you will mess up. The great news is that resilience isn't found in perfection; it's in the repair.

We create a culture of connection in our homes when we know how to repair well. How we handle our children's mistakes will either increase or decrease our connection with them. When your child lies to you, or makes a bad choice, it's easy to get upset.

I once caught my son in a lie to me. He apologized, but every part of me wanted to yell at him. I felt betrayed and wondered if I could ever believe him again, but instead, I forgave him, and said, "Son, today, I am using my faith to trust you."

It's unrealistic to think that our kids will never lie to us or make unwise decisions. My son can't bear the thought of me not trusting him. He needs to learn that trust is earned, but he also needs to learn that home is a place where connection builds when we forgive and choose to trust again, and that there will still be connection when we make mistakes.

Forgiveness is one of the most freeing gifts we can give someone else. Offering forgiveness doesn't mean that what happened was okay. It means releasing ourselves and the other person from blame and the need for retribution ("someone must pay!").

My children are forever messing up and apologizing. So much so that the words, "I'm sorry" really grate on my nerves. They often hear me say, "Saying sorry isn't good enough, so what are you going to do to fix it?"

Sounds fair, right?

I was getting tired of my children purposefully making mistakes and using, "I'm sorry" as a get-out-of-jail-free card. However, I was humbled one time when I was the one who messed up and came to my children to say, "I'm sorry." They put their arms around me and said, "It's okay, Mom. We forgive you." Those words soothed me. I was feeling awful, but when they said they forgave me, I felt beautiful freedom. That day, I realized how wonderful it is to be forgiven.

I'm so glad my children didn't turn to me to say, "Well, saying sorry isn't good enough. What are you going to do to fix it?" That would have made me feel small and shamed. I ate some serious humble pie that day and have taken with me the lesson of releasing people from my someone-needs-to-pay-for-this prison. Apologizing is only the beginning of repair. Offering forgiveness is where the repair really happens.

When there has been a rupture, an argument, or something that has brought disconnection between you and your child, it's important that you initiate the repair—even if you're in the right and they're in the wrong. When we make our kids come to wallow at our feet for their mistakes, it brings much shame to their little hearts. Remember, we're the adults. We lead the way to teach them how relationships work, and healthy ways to handle conflict. When we approach our children to repair the relationship after a mishap, we teach them what connection feels like. It's even more powerful when we do this when they are clearly in the wrong. It reminds them that home is safe, that they can make mistakes, and that nothing will separate them from you.

For many years, I've hated Mother's Day. Before children, I imagined Mother's Day as breakfast in bed and endless praises of children, but now, after having children, this is what it actually looks like:

My youngest wakes up. Dad says, "Go give Mom a hug and say Happy Mother's Day."

He gives me a big hug but instead says, "I can't wait for Grandma to come over today!"

The preteen sluggishly arises and, through his yawn, proclaims, "I *am* your present."

This is real Mother's Day, friends. The worst things in our home seem to happen every year on Mother's Day. My youngest, when he was two years old, smashed our living room window on Mother's Day. My children save the grumpiest versions of themselves for Mother's Day. Each Mother's Day ends the same—Mom crying in the bedroom with all her boys, including her husband, looking bewildered. Husband pushes the children into the bedroom to go apologize. I hear him uttering threats of taking away their video games if they don't. Great. Now saying sorry is a chore. Kids shuffle in with a mediocre "sorry" and I begin to wallow in my self-pity, moaning, "Why can't one day just be about meeee?"

What's interesting is that now my children also hate Mother's Day. When Mother's Day starts creeping up, everyone in our home feels the same anxiety. *How will they mess it up this year?* I'm wondering, and they're scared out of their minds that they'll mess it up. Guess what? They're going to mess it up! They're going to mess it up because, well, they're kids.

One year, when I saw the anxiety creeping into my children as Mother's Day approached, I woke up. *What have I done?* Making my children come to me while I cried on my bed after yet another "horrible" Mother's Day had filled my children's hearts with shame. I made them feel awful. This did the opposite of what I desired. It didn't make them want to show their love for me; it made them *fear* me.

This past Mother's Day, I wrote myself a note and posted it everywhere I could see it: "Your children owe you nothing." It's true. They don't. I set them free of my expectations, and we had the most lovely Mother's Day we've ever experienced. Forgiveness is setting people free from our expectations.

Parents and children have different agendas that can create small or large arguments that can potentially disconnect us. It's important for us to understand what's going on underneath our reactions, and how we're contributing to any disconnection with our children. Remember to check in with yourself about the story you're telling yourself.

I use this often to check myself when my children hurt me. This helps me keep their behaviour in perspective, rather than getting offended. Feeling misunderstood is the number-one way for people to feel disconnected. When I tell myself a story about my child that makes either them or me feel misunderstood, the result is disconnection. When we have too many misunderstandings, we move towards isolation—even while living in the same house. When there is disconnection, the mind becomes disorganized, and the heart then breaks. Connection is vital for emotional wellbeing.

Disconnections are a normal part of any relationship. When disconnection happens, it's important to repair sooner rather than later—not *too* soon, when emotions are high, but when everyone has had a chance to calm down. Putting ourselves in our children's shoes to see the experience through their eyes is a great benefit to repairing disconnection. Even if they're in the wrong, we can explain what the experience must have been like from their point of view without condoning the behaviour.

When we take time to reflect on the emotional experience of a rupture with our child, we are helping them make sense of their story while creating greater connection with them than we had before. Remember all that work you did at the beginning of this book, making sense of your story? Imagine you could help your child process ruptures now. These heartaches can become a catalyst to deepen the relationship. Think about it. Whose parent ever sits down with them after an argument to talk about one another's points of view? Who does that?

In the midst of a rising argument, avoid attempting to reason with your child. Abort mission! When emotions are high, you and your child are in the back of your brain and all sense of reason is shut down. We can get caught up in arguments with our children, whose number-one goal is to convince us to give them whatever they want. Our children need to understand that just because we repair doesn't mean we're giving in to their wishes. We can communicate this in a firm but kind way rather than yelling at them.

Shame is on overdrive when there are ruptures. For example, when our children misbehave in public, we're naturally embarrassed. That's a public rupture we need to repair. If we don't, that child might come to feel both shame and humiliation. These feelings cause our children to turn away from us and others, and have the belief there's something wrong with them, which can shape the development of their personality.

I've seen this happen firsthand with my son. He isolates when he feels shame. There was a season when he felt misunderstood by us and his teachers for a few months. I noticed him shrink and become more alone, wanting to be in his room or close himself off with his video games. He started to believe he was just a "bad kid." I can't repair a rupture experienced with a teacher, but I can change his environment (hence the homeschooling).

As long as I can do my part to continue to repair the relationship, he has a chance to believe that he's worth fighting for. When we don't take time to listen to our children to help them feel understood, it leads to more arguments, which, ironically, leads to further disconnection, which isn't what anyone wants. We all want connection. In order to have it, we have to be empathetic with our children.

How do we repair? We first need to take some space to get perspective on what happened. Not all ruptures can be repaired right away. You might want to go for a walk or even go to a different room to calm yourself down. I use this time to think about why I reacted the way I did. What was underneath the way I responded? Once you're calm, and your child is ready, make the first move to connect. It's important not to think your child will suddenly "get over it."

Timing is also important. If your child has no interest in repair, don't give up. Trust me, your child wants more than anything to be back in relationship with you. Give them the space they need to calm themselves as well.

Do. Not. Blame.

Initiating repair doesn't start with "I'm sorry we had that blow-up, but if you would have just…" Blame and defending ourselves gets us nowhere. This is true for any relationship. It's important for our children to see us taking responsibility for our own reactions and behaviours.

For example, "I'm sorry we had that blow-up. I notice I get worked up easily when I come home from work and see the house is a mess. I need to work on this. I can see how you must have felt when I got upset at you for not cleaning. I could have approached this differently. Will you forgive me?"

Think about how you normally deal with a rupture. We all have ways we naturally deal with fractures in relationships. For example, we might not say sorry until *they* say sorry, or we give our children the silent treatment, or we yell because we feel angry and hurt. How you repair ruptures is key to the resilience your children and family will have.

Now think about how you would *like* to respond to ruptures. Write it out. Often, if we plan what we will do ahead of circumstances we know will arise, we see more desirable outcomes compared to when we react.

We teach our children to repair when we make connection—not being right—our goal, when we're willing to apologize, and when we empathize with how they feel so they feel understood. It's also a good idea to model naming what we can do differently next time so they learn to do this as well. Remember, nothing is ever hopeless. No one is a perfect parent. Our hope is in how we repair. That creates resilience.

Chapter Nineteen
Your Family Is Your Feedback

I WAS ASKED, "WHAT'S THE GREATEST ADVICE YOU WOULD GIVE TO A PARENT?"

"Your family is your feedback," I replied.

Nothing has ever given me greater feedback on how I'm doing as a partner and a parent other than my family. If I'm letting stress get to me or I'm off-balance, my family will soon let me know, mostly through their behaviours. As great as having parenting tools are, nothing will give you better feedback than noticing rises and falls in your child's willingness or unwillingness to connect with you. You will notice negative or positive behaviours and attitudes, and the number of ruptures you have. Listening to these will communicate to you how things are going. These will let you know if you're working too much, if you're giving the kids too much screen time, as well as the level of trust they have with you. They'll let you know if you have enough structure or too much.

It's important to listen to the rhythm of your family. What are your children's behaviours trying to communicate? What are your partner's needs in the moment? Are you listening and responding? I have had to slow down my life many times to stop, listen, and reflect and change. Our willingness to do this will determine the health of our family.

There's no right or wrong way to do this. Adjust to the rhythm of your family. Sit beside your child, rather than across; make connection your priority over changing behaviour; and own your behaviours and reactions first so your child can own theirs. Keep your family values front and centre when giving and listening to feedback so you can move forward into those values together. Avoid comparing yourself and your family to others. If we are wise, humble, and vulnerable, we will listen to the feedback our family gives us.

Youth are a mirror of our culture. How they behave, how they think, what they say mirrors back to us what we've invested into them. With all the mental health and behavioural issues we see in homes and schools, we need to invest better. We need to create spaces where our children know they are courageous. In order to do this, we need to be living lives of vulnerable courage as a model to show them a better story.

Conclusion

THE GREATEST THING I'VE DISCOVERED IN THE JOURNEY FROM MY SON'S MENTAL HEALTH crisis to now is that we all want connection, but don't know how.

After one of the live seminar versions of this book I hosted, a lady put her hand up and asked, "I feel like you haven't given us any tools. How did you get your son out of his mental prison?"

"Everything I just explained is how," I responded. "Making sense of our own story, getting underneath our children's behaviour, letting go of trying to control them, understanding opposition, ADHD, and anxiety, working on my marriage, getting clear on my values, structuring my life, learning to regulate myself, and how to repair. That's what I did."

She still didn't get it.

People today want to know how to connect, but they still think the answers are in diet, counselling, and mindfulness practices alone. I use these three specific examples because they're the ones I hear the most often.

"But what about gluten? Should I take my child off gluten?"

"What about counselling?"

"Should I teach my child mindfulness practices?"

These are good questions to ask, but remember, they are the twenty percent. Eighty percent of your success will come from what I've discussed throughout in this book, based on connection—bringing your child closer—and then when you add all these other elements, they will have a greater impact. It's the harder road, but it's changed my son, my family, and most of all, myself.

I am out to change the mental health game. It's time. The greatest awakening I experienced through my son's crisis is that our children are suffering—needlessly. That was the greatest awakening. If my son can experience healing and breakthrough, so can your child. If I can be brave to face my story to write a better one for my family, so can you. Diagnoses show our vulnerability, but they don't dictate who we are. We aren't broken; rather, society is broken. Our culture is broken. So I say we create some new culture. What if changing ourselves and the way we live could be seen as a prescription that could cure the diagnosis of disconnection?

Don't ever think, "I'm just a parent." When you keep the connection with your kids strong you can say,

"I'm a parent preventing homelessness."

"I'm a parent creating a culture of empathy that can end bullying, self-harm, and suicide."

"I'm a mom and I'm creating a strong generation that will have healthy attachments rather than addictions."

"I'm a parent and I'm making a way for confident, innovative leaders to rise up."

You are not "just a parent." You are playing an enormous role in social change that is needed. We need you.

I would love to connect with you. Let me know how your practices of the principles of this book are going. I would love to visit your city with the seminar version of this book. I also do personal coaching on any aspect of what I have written in this book. If you're needing extra help, reach out to me by emailing me at culturerebelonline@gmail.com. You can also find further tips on my blog at conniejakab.com. You can also find my other books on my website.

Until next time, parents, stay strong. Keep connection with your children always at the centre and know there is more hope than you know waiting for you.

I'm cheering for you.